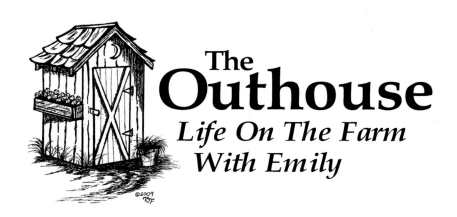

The **Outhouse**
Life On The Farm
With Emily

©2009
TJF

Tammy J. Finney

Tammy Finney
3/17/10

Published by Ridgetop Ranch

Edited by Heidi Mann, Final Touch Proofreading & Editing
Graphic Design/Layout by Gregory Mann, MonkeyMind Studios

To order books, send check or money order for $14.00 per book to cover
costs, tax and shipping to:

Ridgetop Ranch

PO Box 264

Georgetown, MN 56546-0264

EmilysOuthouse@aol.com

Gratitude

A few "acknowledgments" to the troops. Thank you to...

Ed (Wayne): Thanks for being a good sport and a great husband when I've used our escapades in print... Also for the "get 'er done" nudges to publish this book—"our book."

Brandy (Bette): Couldn't have done it without you and your "Atta Gal's." Best always, to my best friend!

John Kolness: for saying, "You wrote one; now you have to keep going." Cheers to the world's greatest boss and friend.

Tom Pantera: I still don't believe a word you say after you edit my columns and state, "Another great one." Thanks for the shoulder to lean on and for teaching me the basics.

Greg and Heidi Mann: What an awesome team! Your talents and hard work to put this book together are much appreciated! Thanks, Greg, for lending your incredible skills for the layout and design. Thanks, Heidi, for stepping in when I was lost to edit, proofread, and organize the whole shebang!

Larry Gauper: for your honest advice and thumbs up.

Tom Blair: for the rebellious partnership we share in writing.

Soo Asheim: for welcoming me into your world.

Shawn Dietrich and Dennis Ding: for your much valued support and friendship.

Brad Stephenson: Thanks for believing in me, for the little "pushes" to believe in myself each time I visited your bookstore, and for the final proofread.

Bridget, living a parallel world with Emily: For asking a hundred times, "When might we see the 'Outhouse' book in print?"—the first copy is yours!

Can't forget Lucy, the "Boy Named Sue," whose feline company I've relied on through all the ups and downs of writing the "Outhouse" columns.

This book is dedicated to the memory of Bev Quam, whose enjoyment of "Emily's Outhouse" put a huge smile on both our faces every Friday.

And last but not least, thanks, Mom!

Table of Contents

Foreword   1
"Honey, I Need a Pull"   2
Don't Fence Me In   4
Welding in 3-D   6
"Whoa, Horse, Whoaaaaaaaaaa!!!"   8
Press One for Japan   10
Don't Shoot the Goat!   12
"Howdy!"   14
Equine IQ   16
Prohibition   18
Jiffy Parts   20
Beware of Cat   22
Sp-rrrrrr-ing?   24
Service Engine Soon   26
Away in the Manger   28
Pigs Don't Have Necks   30
Stanley   32
Daze n Nights   34
Union Rules   36
Complicated Competition   38
Creepy Crawlers   40
Taken for a Ride   42
Moose Among Us   44
Going, Going, Gone   46
Tomfoolery   48
Los Angeles Visits the Farm   50
Westward Ho   52
Got Milk?   54
Traveling with Garmin
Part 1: Continental Divide   56
Part 2: Divide and Conquer   58
Part 3: Divided by Three   60
Trailer Backing – 101   62
Close the Door   64
Communication Gap   66
Textbook of Tricks   68
Prairiewood Condominiums   70

Seasonal Disorganization   72
Soup or Salad?   74
Hey, Mom   76
Three's a Crowd   78
Sidetracked   80
How'd That Happen?   82
Try This, Charlie   84
Off the Farm   86
Lady Buggers   88
Snow Angels   90
"Honey, I Shrunk the Barn"   92
Resolution   94
Calamity Janes   96
The Color Purple   98
Good Morning, Wilbur   100
Color Blind   102
Techno-Drama   104
Smokey the Bear   106
"Dear Mom…"   108
Necessities   110
Party On   112
Treasure Hunt   114
For the Record   116
Camels Have Humps; Llamas Don't   118
Dry Clean Only   120
Concealed by Default   122
Captain Crunch-Berries Strikes Again   124
"You're Hired"   126
Don't Want It All   128
Snowed In   130
Barn in a Bag   132
Lifeguard on Duty   134
Drivability   136
General Hospital   138
Written in Stone   140
"Dear Dad…"   142

Foreword

A friend of mine once summed up Tammy Finney's writing thus: "She could make dirt interesting."

I found out later that in one of her columns she, in fact, has done just that.

Tammy is our most popular columnist at The FM Extra newspaper. When I found that out, I couldn't have been less surprised. Among her many gifts is an ability most columnists would kill for: a talent for making the reader feel like he's sitting across from her over coffee and just shooting the breeze. The rest of us who have columns here have certain hobbyhorses we ride and our audiences are pretty specific. But everybody can dig what Tammy writes about. She talks in her inimitable style about the small frustrations and tiny triumphs of daily life. Her columns ring a bell with both the ditch digger and the bank president.

And as someone who's made a living both practicing and teaching writing, I can tell you that Tammy is the best natural writer I've ever known. Reading her stuff, you'd never know she sweats blood over every word. In the first place, her worst ideas are better than the best ideas many of us have. And nearly every time I edit her column, I find a little, gem-like surprise nestled somewhere: something that's said just right and — bonus! — makes me chuckle.

I've told her all this, and her greatest charm is that she doesn't quite believe it. I've never met someone whose talent comes with so little ego.

So, get that cup of coffee, sit back and spend some time with our Emily.

Tom Pantera
Managing Editor
Extra Media, Inc.
Moorhead, Minn.

"Honey, I Need a Pull"

The first Tuesday of each month has always been vegetable beef soup day. If Christmas or any other holiday happened to fall on that particular day of the week, homemade soup was served as the main course with a side order of turkey, ham, or red, white, and blue burgers.

Mom had her order of things down pat when preparing her delicious dish, and it was the one Betty Crocker staple that I actually learned to cook well.

Timing was everything in the five-hour start-to-finish process. Jobs around the house could be done in between the meat-simmering and vegetable-peeling, but a pot not watched turned into a wicked, wicked meal.

When bounced on the kitchen counter, the tester dumpling didn't quite make the required six-inch rebound, meaning the kettle of goodies was about a half-hour from perfection. "As the World Turns" was tuning in and it was a good day…

Holly had received the news of an incurable disease and I wiped tears away as I answered the phone during a commercial. The words "Honey, I need a pull" made me bawl out loud and curse the day I married a farmer.

Ed said it would only take a minute or two—oh, sure, just like the last technical difficulty he got himself into that's still out in the mud somewhere! As I scrambled for an excuse of any kind, Ed used the silence on my end of the phone to give directions to the field he was in and to tell me to bring along the extra-heavy log chain and long-handled spade.

Weighing the two options of chef's-delight soup or a very angry husband buried in mud, I repeated our wedding vows out loud to myself, emphasizing the word "worse" as I walked out the door, pouring our Tuesday evening meal into the dog dish.

The scene was just as I had expected. The top half of the tractor was visible, which was a good thing, but Ed's hat was torn in half and I didn't dare ask on what part of the planet he had left the field cultivator.

Getting out of the pickup, I repeated to myself the word "better" over and over again as the situation most certainly could not get any worse.

Innocently thinking I had nothing to do with the big fat muddy mess in the field, I guess I was terribly wrong; while peeling the potatoes for the soup, somehow I had steered the tractor toward the mud hole at the same time!

I didn't dare say "Triple A" out loud — that would have ended my life — but I did sneak in a funny about digging down to China for the rest of the tractor, making sure all the while that Ed had enough mud on his boots so he couldn't move and that his hands were empty of wife-threatening objects.

"Put it in four low, and when I wave, floor it."

At this point of no return, I'm hooked to ten tons of steel, and for a slight instant I imagine a happy-go-lucky fellow at the controls of the tractor, wearing a suit from "Green Acres." Stupidly, I start humming the song. I guess I missed the "wave" as my cheerful little jingle was rudely interrupted by a hammer crashing into the back windshield of the pickup.

Wishing the truck came equipped with an "eject" button, I would have gladly pressed it even if the directions stated "no parachute connected; you will land on your head."

With teeth clenched, I tapped out the "Green Acres" jingle on the steering wheel with my thumbs while staring into the rearview mirror, holding my breath, and waiting for instructions.

The "floor it" wave commenced, looking more like a one-armed, high-speed windshield wiper than a "please pull me out of this mess, honey; I'm an idiot."

Just like all the other pulls and right on track, the pickup slid sideways, and of, course, it was because my wheels were turned in the wrong direction.

What was left of Ed's hat was now torn into little-bitty shreds as he made a disgruntled counter-circling direction with both arms, like all the other times I crapshooted the start of a pull.

With wheels facing the proper direction, the pull was in motion once again, only this time I really feared for my life as the mud and smoke from the pickup tires limited my view to the little Hawaiian dancer on the dash. With white knuckles on the steering wheel, I could feel the truck moving and quickly planned my own funeral if or when the two hundred horses under the tractor's hood reached solid ground before I did.

Pulling the happy little dancer off the dash and tossing her out the window made me feel a whole lot better when everything had come to a stop and both machines had completed their mud wrestling for the day.

Ed unhooked the chain without a glance up, down, or sideways to acknowledge that Emily had saved the day.

Over chicken pot pies for supper, we both laughed at the dog, wondering how he could eat the entire pot of soup and leave every carrot untouched. No words will ever be spoken out loud about pulls, as it would result in thousands of wifeless farmers.

I fully intend to call the telephone company one of these days to install caller ID for "Honey, I need a pull"…

Don't Fence Me In

I was informed we would be fencing the next weekend and was soooo looking forward to about it—about as much as a root canal. This particular fencing project was for cattle, so it needed to be built tall, strong, straight as an arrow, and made of bull-proof wire. Ed would do the instructing, as he was the professional fence architect, and my title was "runner" because we all know girls don't know a thing about putting up a proper fence. I wouldn't hold the tape correctly so a post or two would be off by an inch and we would have to re-do it. The wood ticks would get me, so a hissy fit or two would take place. The wire I unwrap and do not hold tight enough will turn into the world's largest slinky, and the posts I counted the day before will come up short by ten or twenty.

Hee hee, I will then be instructed with nasty verbiage and flailing arms to run into town for more posts, and I'll sneak a little pre-planned side trip to the Dairy Queen and Herberger's with the previous day's clipped coupons in my back pocket, getting home way too late to finish the project by dark.

Whatever happened to the single-wire electric fence with sheets torn up in little strips and tied between each post to make it visible? Speaking of posts, I miss the skinny little electric fence posts that you can push into the ground with a tennis shoe or rubber boot and pull back out with one hand tied behind your back. The whole fence could be picked up, wrapped up, and moved in a matter of a few minutes for fresh grazing.

I suppose the "flags" are too expensive nowadays, having to cut up 700-thread-count pure Egyptian cotton sheets, or maybe our modern-bred animals don't see as well as they used to. Heck, in the good old days we would picket our horses out to graze by tying the end of a long rope to a cement block. The horse would munch a little bit, then pull a little bit and never wander too far away, with the smaller ones making precise little crop circles as they weren't strong enough to pull the block more than a few feet.

One time we had three or four horses staked out in this incredibly uncomplicated way when a neighbor's plastic kiddy pool was blown by the wind and rolled down the road straight toward our farm. Cement blocks can bounce pretty dang high when being dragged through a plowed field at forty miles an hour behind a terrified horse.

The selection of fencing materials is absurd nowadays: cattle panels, horse panels, hog panels, sheep panels, but I think they still call chicken wire "wire." When did we get so specialized with our fencing? Then, of course, we must pick the thickness gauge of our new animal enclosure. Let's see, if I have a thousand-pound horse, does it require five-, 10-, or 15-gauge wire?

We tried using electric fence for the hogs one time. The problem is, hogs root in the dirt and don't look up to smell the wire (yes, animals can smell the electricity; wish I could, but that's a whole other story), and electric wire cannot be strung close to the ground or it'll short out. By the time the pig's shoulders touch the fence to get a shock, they are long gone. "The pigs are out" is one of those calls that really, really wrecks your day.

I did assemble a cute little decorative wood fence along our sidewalk one summer. I cast off all offers of help from Ed; this building project was close to the house and in "my territory." I had no clue how hard it was to dig with a hand posthole digger, measuring down with a yardstick every few turns for post depth, waiting for the dang oil to start gushing out! Receiving the "I told you so" look every morning when Ed walked out of the house as I tweaked my pile of lumber, there was no way I was going to let him touch one teeny-tiny nail or board, even as he tossed the words over his shoulder, "That's gonna take you a coon's age to build."

One very fortunate day, the Schwan's man pulled in for a delivery as I was sitting on the edge of a posthole, looking down and waiting for a fellow from China to crawl up and help me out.

We negotiated a small butcher hog for labor, and the jolly fellow dug right in. In no time at all we had each posthole measured to perfect specifications.

Later that afternoon, the UPS attendant arrived with a package from Great-Aunt Ida. In a whirlwind of trading, half of Aunt Ida's homemade peanut butter cookies left with the big brown truck and my fence boards were nailed on straight as an arrow.

Coming off the school bus, the kids jumped for joy as I handed each a paintbrush with instructions to have a war with one child placed on either side of the rails.

Humph, who was it who said gals couldn't build a perfect fence in no time at all...

Welding in 3-D

A couple of years ago I stopped in the shop to ask Ed something and waited in line with the dog as he was busy welding some gates together. From the day we could walk, we were taught to look away when a person was welding so your eyes wouldn't be burned, and as I turned around and asked my question to the wall, I received as much response from Ed as I did from it.

Hanging by the door was an extra welding helmet, so I thought, "Hmmm… let's put this on and scope out the miracles of ironwork that have been constructed behind my back for years and years."

Well, Holy Moly, this was by far the best crafting project I'd ever seen! Paint-by-number was written all over it and scrapbooking was instantly obsolete. "May I?" was answered with a raised eyebrow, indicating that Ed knew, "I better let her try or there won't be supper for a week."

Impatiently given the one, two, three-step instructions, I was left, to my heart's delight, with fifty feet of iron and a can of welding rods. Finding out immediately that the welding craft was a bit more of a challenge than I had thought, I couldn't quit before starting, as the "I told you so's" would be heard for a month.

Navigating the invisible barrier between the welding rod and the iron to get the two working smoothly together was a major undertaking. Striking too close and fast, the rod was stuck like super glue to the gate, and a slow swipe melted the rod right into the cement floor (oops). After about the hundredth try and half the afternoon, I was well on my way; they would be calling me soon from Europe to fly over and repair the Leaning Tower of Pisa!

Uh oh! Something was burning and it wasn't the iron. My dang shirtsleeve was on fire! Stopping, dropping, and rolling was out of the question as we diehard welders could take a little pain, but thank goodness I had remembered to engage instruction step number three: "Put on the welding gloves."

Now a professional welder, I was having a blast creating little twirls of melted iron all along the gate. Designing my initials into the end while patting myself on the back, I stood up and proudly surveyed the art project of the century. I mulled over the notion of patenting my technique; as far as I was concerned, it was unequaled and far surpassed any others in the whole county!

Ed walked in as I was lounging on a stool, and just as I was asking if he wanted my autograph, he picked the gate up off the floor and it came apart in ten or so pieces. "This can't be happening," I thought to myself. "He's just jealous of my workmanship and wrecking it on purpose!" I was the Welding Goddess and this gate was built stronger than a Mac truck.

Watching my pretty little welds falling apart one by one, I tried to save face by telling Ed my project wasn't finished yet and to "leave it alone!"

Ed started laughing as he held up the corner branded with my initials, not realizing he was sinking deeper and deeper into the wrath of Emily. "FINE, do it yourself then!" I said, wishing I could slam the overhead door on the way out while thinking of a few good "paybacks."

Still laughing, Ed yelled, "Hey, what did you want to ask me earlier?" I replied, "Oh, just if you would come up to the house and thread my sewing machine." Ha! — last laughs are best as I imagined him trying to tackle that modus operandi...

"Whoa, Horse, Whoaaaaaaaaaa!!!"

Remember our first ponies? The ones that were so sweet and innocent until you got within fifty feet of them? I was extremely lucky to have the perfect first pony. Pinky was a gem and a confidence-builder, allowing me to have a false base of trust and security with all horses ever after. When, sadly, I'd outgrown Pinky, we went shopping for the next well-trained, wonderful steed.

Ranger was found a few miles away. The chaw-chewing, bow-legged, spur-twirling seller said, "Yaa, this here horse is just what yer looking for. He's a been-there, done-that, broker-than-broke gelding, and if you don't like him, I'll take him back and give you a refund." Well, how could we go wrong? As a young teen, I was immediately smitten with this animal. He was far more beautiful than Black Beauty and could surely outrun Secretariat.

The deal was done before loading Ranger into the trailer. Oooops, Ranger didn't like the trailer too well. That's OK, I could ride him home. Oooops, we forgot to try out Ranger's road smarts on the test drive. Quickly finding out that I owned a hunter-jumper in disguise, I made it home on a cross-country tour well before Mom and Dad pulled in. Stubborn young gals will never admit defeat, even if our legs were shaking so bad getting off the horse that it was impossible to walk.

On Ranger's "good" days he would allow me to catch him for a wishful ride. Saddling the good old boy was a skill; everything had to be done from the exact middle of his side so he couldn't reach around to bite me or cow-kick with his hind leg. Getting on from the fence was a balancing act, and the first and last time I tried from the ground resulted in Ranger steeple-chasing by himself across the country with the saddle hanging under his belly and me following with the bucket of grain. I concluded this animal was born on the sixth day of the sixth month of the sixth year; he was indeed the Devil incarnate!

Not remembering what appliance came in the big sturdy cardboard box but seeing it sitting empty outside the house, I imagined the "perfect horse-drawn sleigh." It didn't take long to braid up some twine and fit ol' Ranger with a nice harness. Not thinking ahead to an "escape route," I tied the makeshift harness around the box two or three times and then around the horse four or five times. Ranger stood quietly throughout the "hooking up" stage, and I was dreaming of a nice sleigh ride through Central Park.

A five-gallon pail fit tidily inside the box for a perfect seat, and Ranger was asked for a "walk on." It was "all she wrote" when the rope tightened and the box slid right into his rear end. For a brief moment I was an Egyptian Princess and Ben Hur was driving his chariot beside me, but reality set in real fast as the box became airborne and Ranger went from one to fifty miles per hour in four hoof beats.

We had made it across the yard when the fancy chariot made a U-turn toward the house. I had lost my pail on the first jump and was on my knees, hanging onto the sides of the box for dear life.

Turning the corner, Ranger made it around the sliding glass doors of the patio ever so daintily, but the chariot and I shined up the glass pretty good. Taking the doors out was only the first "tornado alley" of destruction that we left behind that afternoon. Ranger and I managed to tear down the clothesline, flatten the doghouse, and chase my very infuriated father halfway down the driveway. Getting "hooked" on the pickup bumper on the last trip around the farm, we tore half of that off before my "sleigh" finally broke apart and we slowed to a bumpy halt.

If we still had a doghouse, I would have been required to sleep in it for a very long time after my little sleigh ride excursion.

Regretfully, Ranger was returned to the seller and the bow-legged chaw-chewer was "delighted" when told his sweet old gelding was now a well-trained, been-there, done-that driving horse...

Press One for Japan

Yep, I'm a neat freak when it comes to mowing the yard. My motto is "If you're not going to weed-whack afterwards, don't bother mowing." At least then the whole works will be even.

On Mother's Day a few years ago I was presented with the most wonderful gift ever—a powerful, brand spankin' new weed-whacker. Ryobi cut to a tee, taking down everything from the finest grasses to small trees in one single swipe.

Over the years Ryobi has gotten pretty particular about starting and staying running. Four and one-half presses of the primer with full choke, let it rest for 3.2 seconds. While holding the throttle between one-fourth and a half, it needs three-fourths of a choke and then full throttle while shutting the choke down—all the while pulling the rip cord constantly, or should I say "arm ripper-offer" for short. After about an hour, Ryobi starts to spit and sputter, so a tilt to the left for three minutes while using half-throttle is in order.

Last weekend all was going well with the mowing progress until it was Ryobi's turn for cleanup. We've had our small arguments in the past but always came to an agreement that Ryobi would straighten out and get the job done to Emily's standards. First the string ran out—no problem, a five-minute replacement procedure.

Oops—"problem" after all: the arrow that shows where to place the round thing at the bottom that you line up to stick the string into had worn off and it was luck of the draw. Gently place the string in, half-click counterclockwise… nope. Try again: place the string in the next hole and pray a bit… nope. Shove the string down Ryobi's throat and scream.

One hour and ten minutes later, Ryobi is efficiently re-strung.

Bad news: we're out of gas and the weed-whacker gas can is empty. No problem; drive to the neighbor's two miles away and borrow some. No one's home, but the dog invites you into the garage and shows you where the container marked "weed-whacker gas" is. Good dog.

With a full layer of string and a plumb-full gas tank, we're ready to go again. The breeze goes down and the gnats come lurking, so weed-whack with one hand and brush the bugs off with the other. Switch arms when

10

one gets tired and smack yourself in the face when aiming for the neck because that arm is used to holding twenty pounds of Ryobi.

After taking a "power break" and dousing with bug spray, I resumed the trimming procedure with huge hopes of finishing before supper. One clunk and a "tizinggg" dashed all hopes of a smooth ending; Ryobi had a screw loose someplace inside the engine. Getting the machine apart and finding the screw was a whole lot easier than figuring out where the screw came from and putting it back together. Ed was in the field and screening all enraged Ryobi calls, so I figured the manual would give me directions to place the screw in its proper position. Problem: no manual. Light bulb: I could find it on the Internet.

The first thing I learned is that no one in California is allowed to purchase Ryobis as it would add to the state's pollution (poor fellas). The next thing I learned was that I needed a model number, and that was the second thing to wear off after the arrow for the strings.

The 1-800 help line was impressively supportive: "We are here to assist you between the hours of eight and five, Monday through Friday." Don't people usually mow on the weekends?

Fifteen screens deep on the computer, I found photos! There was my Ryobi, with links for parts and manuals. Yahoooo! Crap, guess what? All links had been abandoned because my Ryobi model was extinct, but they did have a wish list link available. At this point in time no one at the Ryobi company would care to hear my wishes upon them.

On the top of the page was a "video link." I thought, "What the heck"; maybe Hoshi Mashie could be seen putting a Ryobi back together. Nope, this link brought me directly to clips on MySpace! How in the world could I start out looking for a Ryobi manual and end up viewing a bizarre college fraternity party?

It was about midnight and I had long since given up any hope of finishing my weed-whacking, but there sure were some interesting visual manuals on MySpace...

Don't Shoot the Goat!

I had heard somewhere that goats were great companions for horses, so I thought I'd give it a try. Common sense said no, but this one was sooo cute!

Sweet little goat was delivered and placed in the horse barn while I was away on errands for the day. Previous "keep your mouth shut and don't say a word until cash is in your hand" goat owner didn't bother to tell me anything about goats, especially the fact that they viewed horse tails as a delicacy.

Arriving home, I found four horses with nicely squared-off, considerably shorter tails. Goat had a look on her face that said, "Only their hair dresser could tell for sure." Swallowing her excuse while double-thinking my sanity, I petted cute little goat and welcomed her to her new home, silently praying that the horses' tails would grow out before anyone noticed.

Ed came over to "my side" of the farm to see the new little pet and, on his way out the door, laughed and said my horses looked like a bunch of jackasses with the short tails. I made a mental note to dunk his toothbrush in the toilet.

Goat needed to be halter-broke and the Yellow Pages omitted any listing for goat trainers. Standing in separate corners of the horse stall, the two of us squared off and stared eye-to-eye, questioning who was going to train whom.

I decided to try the method used on horses where the animal is moved around in a circle until a little tired and then is supposed to come on in and "join up" with the trainer. Well, Goat joined up all right, right on top of me! As I was lying in the horse poop, I drew the conclusion that what was underneath me was considerably better smelling than what was on top of me. Goats stink — I mean, really stink!

Eventually Goat adopted me as her number-one person while accepting the collar and lead. She did most of the leading while I followed.

Goat was protector of Emily. Where I went, she went. No horse, dog, or human was to come close or she would stand on her back legs and tilt her head while using her fifty-pound body as a battering ram. I was quite fond of my little bodyguard, but Ed wasn't too impressed when her horns started growing and he got it in the rump a few times after coming too close to our happy little circle. The UPS worker hung our packages on the mailbox at the end of the driveway, and we received a nasty letter with an invoice attached for a new pair of delivery driver trousers.

Goat had great fun practicing mountain climbing on Ed's pickup hood, and I didn't see much need to reprimand her for it as the truck was old and scratched-up anyways. The day she saw her reflection in the windshield ended a little dicey as the "other" goat was battered beyond repair and Ed needed a new windshield.

It was time to corral the goat or, as Ed nicely stated, "Keep that four-legged destruction varmint penned up, or it's open goat-shooting season on the farm."

Christmas was just around the corner, and our church asked if the yearly tree-cutting hayride could come to our place. One of the young lads came out early that morning, sporting a beautiful pre-cut evergreen, and hid it amongst the trees behind the barn. That afternoon, the wagonload of excited children arrived to chop down a special tree for the Christmas Eve service. I stayed behind, chatting with the minister and his wife while the group trotted into the woods, searching for their tree.

Back came the kids, followed by a goat and a tree that looked like it had been to the spa for a pedicure and major leg wax. Everything was stripped clean as far up as a goat could reach on her hind legs, and I swallowed hard while kicking some rocks around, trying to think of an excuse for my sweet little pet. Goat had that look on her face that said, "Don't you dare take away my pie a la mode."

The kids didn't mind that the bottom half of their tree looked like a naked bird, and the minister was humble about the situation, reaching to shake my hand in thanks for the happy day. Goat saw her morning delicacy being hauled away and the person responsible was way too close to her human. I saw it coming before the minister did and there was no way to stop it. Goat battered him in a spot below his chest and above the knees. His bent-over response came in a slow-motion sentence that resembled what Ralphie blurted out in "A Christmas Story." Twenty-odd children stood in total shock with their eyes and mouths wide open...

"Howdy!"

Turning off the highway and onto a gravel road, you get a "wave" from most everyone you meet. Usually it's a forefinger held up in acknowledgment of the on-coming driver. Sometimes a pinky pops up from those that I consider to have a "sissy" wave or who are just plain too lazy to hold up the proper extremity. I'll admit there've been times I would have liked to keep all fingers down except the "middle" one when greeting a windshield-eating, 100-mph, rock-throwing pickup.

The "four fingers" wave is almost like a hug, a little too personal for me unless it's from a family member.

Five fingers held up or flashing the headlights on and off either means "stop to chat" or "you're driving straight with your blinker on."

No wave at all means someone is having a very bad day or is just plain not friendly. Those persons should drive on the designated "crabby" gravel roads.

I wonder if Eskimos stop their dogs and get off the sleds to rub noses?

Would the Chinese bow and hit their foreheads on the steering wheel?

When meeting or passing a combine or other such large machinery on a narrow gravel road, I never try to make eye contact or give the finger wave; it would mean certain death in the ditch.

Two pickups stopped on the road beside each other means you wait behind them until the guys are done talking. No horn honking allowed on gravel roads; it's not polite. When the conversation is done, the fellow passing you gives a nice "howdy" finger wave.

A few years ago, we had a township resident who did the 100-mph drive-by three or four times a day on the gravel road in front of our farm. We nicknamed him the "screamin' demon," and you could see him coming, followed by his dust cloud, from a mile away. I didn't particularly care for this fellow, and I think the "demon" went out of his way just to dust us and give a "finger wave" as he passed by.

Being the little problem-solver that I was, I thought of a surefire way to slow the "demon" down to settle his dust cloud and protect all living things in his way. "Speed bumps" would do the trick perfectly, I figured, thinking he would have to slow way down to drive over them. It only took a few hours to shovel gravel from the side of the road to the center in three nice, tidy little rows about ten feet apart and six inches high. I patted myself on the back and sat on the picnic table, waiting for the nice slow drive-by.

Poof! — the "demon" hit my stakeout without a glance and gave a "finger wave" I could barely see through his dust.

When one of Emily's ideas is trashed, look out!

It only took a few more hours the next day to cut and drag some small branches from the woods and spread them along the middle of the road for about twenty feet. This was a battle I was going to win, and "demon" would surely have to slow way down to avoid the mess.

Lounging back on the picnic table, sipping coffee, I waited again for the 100-mph duster. Not slowing down a bit, he hit the branches and one flew high enough to take out the mailbox! Ohhhh, was I ticked seeing his slimy little "finger wave" through the back window of the pickup.

I calmed myself down so as not to hide in the ditch the next day with a shotgun. My family thought I was nuts when I took my son's "Buddy Doll" out to the side of the road and propped him up with an electric fence post. Remember "Buddy Dolls"? (They were realistic rag dolls the size of a four-year-old child.) If this didn't slow down "demon," nothing but blood would.

Humming triumph at the picnic table with a side order of coffee cake, I could see the duster speeding down the road towards "Buddy." Choking on a mouthful of cake and spilling hot coffee on my lap, I about fainted when he didn't slow down one single bit and "finger waved" to the doll!

We didn't see too much of "demon" after that dusty day. I suppose he started detouring around our side of the county after seeing the "double middle finger wave" in his rearview mirror by a mad woman chasing his truck down the road while dragging what looked like a four-year-old child by the hair...

Equine IQ

Last Saturday, a friend called saying she was having a terrible time with her horse and wondering if I would come over and help her out. Asking what the problem was, I immediately knew how to "fix" it, but no matter how I flailed my arms and moved my feet over the phone, she just couldn't grasp the concept. Saying "so long" to my afternoon nap and "hello" to equine problem number two zillion, it was off to the rescue. When asked how I knew how to fix the predicament that was simple in my eyes but disastrous in my friend's, I told her it was simple math — been there, done that!

Thinking back to the "beens and dones," it truly is a miracle that I survived the equine learning years. I shudder at the thought of the "theres and thats" yet to come.

One huge lesson that came along by accident — I guess most of the problems were accidents, but some were of the lower human IQ version — was to never, ever tie a horse to a picnic table, no matter how bad you had to pee. You see, horses have this little fleeing instinct that's bred into them that says, "When I pull back and the picnic table moves forward to gobble me up, I'm going to run away from the big brown wooden monster, and when it follows, I'll kick the crap out of it." The high IQ of a horse in that situation is very understandable, while the human scratching her head has to figure out a way to reconstruct the table before her dad comes home.

They say "don't look a gift horse in the mouth." Who listens to "them" anyways? I did, after about the tenth gift of a horse. Remembering the first free equine, I was so thrilled to keep the dollar bills in my pocket that the tidbits of information for Little Miss Freebee went in one ear and out the other. A few allergies, a little lame, but well-broke — and free! I could have paid for Secretariat twice over after all the vet calls and medications. By the time that mare was sound enough to ride, she was too darn old.

On the other side of "free" there's been a few situations when I've questioned my intelligence over and over again. The gelding was a bit spendy, but jet black, and he had a pedigree of champions a mile long.

OK, I will admit the purchase was a bit "my horse is better than your horse," but so what—he was well trained to drive and that was my hobby of the year.

"Think smarter, Emily," as this gorgeous gelding's nickname was Satan. Oh, we looked so dang fancy jogging down the road with my shiny new red cart; I could hardly stand it! Drive on, Satan, drive on... until the quiet country road narrowed and we were face-to-face with a combine with no room to turn around and the only option was a tight pass. Somewhere in the back of my mind, the words whizzed through from the previous owners—"We haven't had him out on the road much"—as my easy-entry, easy-exit cart turned into The Towering Inferno. Watching from the inside of my smashed-to-smithereens cart in the ditch as old Satan's shiny black rear galloped off into the sunset, I could have sworn I caught a glimpse of a brand on his side—a pitchfork and two horns.

Raising colts is a fine extracurricular activity. However, when deciphering the ratio of profit and loss after a few hundred bales of hay and a truckload of oats, we horse enthusiasts sometimes drop off the high-IQ end in a hurry.

Naming him Deno, I caught all kinds of flack, but the ugly little brown colt looked just like a baby dinosaur. One thing this colt took a liking to right off was a beverage of the malted variety. Deno would take the can in his teeth, tip it up, and slurp down every last drop! We had great times in the barn after chores some nights—one for you and one for me. At a year old, Deno had matured into a fine colt with a coat as slick as glass. When the neighbors complimented his glow, I hinted at the secret family recipe of mixed grains.

Off to our first horse show, Deno and I were extremely nervous, so we both "tipped a few" before entering the ring. Since it was a prestigious regional event, the judges were dressed in tuxedos and formals while we paraded around the arena to show our best. When it came our turn to take center stage for conformation, we had to be reminded as both of us were in a world of our own along the rail in the midst of a little burping contest. Long story short, and from someone who's "been there, done that," I ended up in a sprawling heap in the dirt staring at a pair of tuxedo shoes while Deno calmly munched at the hem of a judge's green velvet formal. Infuriated that we were excused from the arena, I announced to the judges in a very high-IQ voice that, in no uncertain terms, they were missing out on the best-looking dinosaur of the whole class...

Prohibition

We didn't mean to cause such a ruckus. The only intention we children had was to brew up a little homemade wine and have a campout.

It was big brother's bright idea to spend our cumulative allowances for an entire month on frozen grape juice that was to be the main staple of our red concoction.

Apparently, our wise older sibling had watched "The Waltons" one too many times and thought John Boy looked pretty dang appropriate sipping Papa's recipe in the company of the Baldwin sisters.

Planning a ways ahead, our brilliant leader coaxed the rest of us to swipe a weekly booty from Mom's kitchen so she wouldn't miss anything.

Yeast was the first item on our list of pilfering, and we girls filled our pockets on bread-making days, stashing our plunder under a board in the chicken house.

The next required component from the kitchen was sugar, and Mom missed her sugar a tish more than her yeast. We girls were questioned more than once about our baking abilities, but with all dishes tasting OK, we were off the hook. Using the "we spilled it" excuse, there were a few close calls, but the designated amount of sweetener was shoplifted from the cupboard.

Big brother was in charge of obtaining the required amount of alcohol. The rest of us siblings never asked or cared where he got it, but one day under the floor boards of the chicken house there appeared a gallon of pure, toxic, 100-proof elixir.

At a community club dinner, each sibling was required to "borrow" a crock pot—easier instructed than carried out. The smorgasbord police stopped us dead in our tracks at the exit. Six children lugging six crock pots out the back door with six different names labeled on them was not the norm. We were saved by quick thinking from elder sister, and the chief apron-wearer of the kitchen helped us kids haul the pots to the back of the pickup, reminding us to thank our mother for bringing them home to wash.

It took two months before Mom and Dad scheduled a trip out of town for the weekend. As we all received our lists of chores to be done, little brother just about blew it when he asked for an extra job title, receiving a very high, suspiciously raised eyebrow from Dad. The pickup wasn't half-ways out the driveway before our mad scramble to the chicken house to collect up the goods for some fine wine making.

Well fermented, the once frozen grape juice smelled a tad vinegary as it was exhumed from the floor boards. Who were we to think months ahead and have a plan to keep a case of juice frozen in the middle of the summer?

With six extension cords plugged into outlets in every corner of the house and threaded out through the windows, we children had a regular distillery brewing in the back yard.

Big brother was in charge of mixing the ingredients as he carefully walked from pot to pot, measuring and pouring while the rest of us looked on in awe, anticipating the taste-testing.

Around nightfall, the lid to the first pot blew off and up way over the pig barn, and it was decided that our brew was finished and ready for consumption.

Saying, "Cheers," big brother poured himself a huge glass and gulped it to the bottom without taste-testing first. Bad, bad mistake as he dropped to the ground with heels up, resembling a fainting goat.

The rest of us sipped and gagged, then sipped and gagged a while longer until we turned blue or just sat down and watched the stars swirl.

Coming to life late the next afternoon with all in complete agreement that homemade wine was not what it was cracked up to be, panic set in as Mom and Dad were expected home within the hour.

Eliminating the evidence was easy; we poured all five-and-a-half gallons of leftover wine in the water tank inside the cow fence. Burying the crock pots behind the wood shed, we figured no one would discover them until we were all old and grey.

As we sat at dinner on Monday, Dad came in late to say the cows were stumbling all over the place and a few of them wouldn't get up off the ground. As the vet was called out for an emergency visit, six children sat around the kitchen table with eyes as big as saucers.

Following a very suspicious father and veterinarian to the cattle barn, all six of us made the excuse that one of our summer FFA projects was to spend some time with a vet. Scratching his head, the doc drew some blood from a couple of the "downed cows" and went on his way. Sighing in relief that we were off the hook, we kids immediately resumed our daily battles.

A few mornings later, we awoke to find the vet report lying on the kitchen table, stating that Dad's cattle were fine but recovering from a very high level of alcohol in their systems. Next to the report were six sparkling clean crock pots and a note from Mom and Dad that they would be back from town later.

Goodnight, John Boy…

Jiffy Parts

OK, Ladies, I know you've all been there and done this, so I'm thinking it's time we unite and unionize ourselves around the age-old myth that the farm wife's third, eighteenth, or twenty-seventh job should be to run for parts.

How did this special selected position ever come to be? Did the Cave Man require his mate to run for a fresh stick because his broke while he was hitting a dinosaur over the head?

What about the Romans? When a chariot broke down, was there a franchise buggy dealer nearby for the spouse to gather parts from?

How about the Sodbusters? By the time the wife lugged the plow piece to the nearest settlement, had it fixed by the blacksmith, and then lugged it back home again, the snow would have been flying.

When I think of it, parts-running must have been so much simpler in any of these previous times of history. How many parts does a "stick" have to screw up the order? Chariots couldn't have had more than two or three. A one-bottom plow only had one bottom.

I detest the little pickups with the hardhats on top; they can weave in and out of traffic so fast, speeding along like little roadrunners with dust behind them on their way for parts. I think there's a hardhat around the farm here somewhere; I should duct-tape it to the top of our one-ton dually and run right over those little peeps. Hee hee, see who's first in line at the parts store then!

"Run in and get a belt for the combine, the pulley belt on the left side of the auger." Does Mr. Farmer have any clue how many belts there are in that area of a combine? I counted about fifteen the last time I peeked inside one. That means a minimum of six trips back and forth to the implement dealer before I bring home the right size belt.

Have you ever been inside one of those shops for a part? The counter fellas see a woman coming from a mile away and conveniently disappear. They need to make a translation book for Mrs. Farmer and Mr. Parts Man. "It's about so long, and it's located above the right wheel, directly below the auger." "What size, year, make, and model?" "You're the dang parts expert; figure it out! In those twenty big fat books on the counter, the belt I need is certainly listed in one of them."

I was sent in once for a wheel — a little wheel for a little feed cart. How hard could that be? Let me tell you how many different sizes of little wheels are hanging on the wall to choose from: A LOT. As I tried to visualize the cart in my mind, zoning in on the wheels and judging what size they were, the kind young salesman asked if I needed help. "Well, if you would simply drive out to our farm, go in the barn and measure the wheels on the feed cart, we'd be all set now, wouldn't we..." I didn't get any more wheel help.

They named the Energizer Bunny after my old John Deere riding lawn mower. Of course, I called him "John" and he was a workaholic, never letting me down. We mowed together for as long as I could remember, even before the kids were born (and that was a long, long time ago). It was six years and seven months ago that John hit a rock on a sunny August afternoon, causing a chain reaction that lasted a half hour. First the blades went flying in all directions like boomerangs but never came back. Then the muffler split in two, causing a small grass fire. Next went the engine, smoking and screaming like nothing I've heard before.

Poor old John was a mess and so was I; how could I ever mow again without him? PARTS! I would take what was left of John to the parts store and they would get him fixed up good as new.

The elderly gentleman at the counter rubbed his jaw and raised an eyebrow as I asked for the proper necessities to fix up my buddy. "Ma'am, we may have the right sized blades, but that's about all I can help you with." Good enough for me; I took the blades and drove to the dealership down the road.

That fellow scratched his head and said, "Sorry, they just don't make 'em like this anymore," but his cousin might have an old engine way, way out back that might work.

The surgery went well, and old John was good as new again. I figured as long as I was at it, I might as well give the old feller a fresh coat of paint. For some reason the John Deere people have some serious dibs on their shade of green, so I thought, what the heck, purple would be a nice change of pace.

I was so dang proud of my very own parts run that ended in such a great way, I fired up old John as soon as we got home and went out to mow. The "cousin from the back room" failed to tell me that "new" John was implanted with a 30-horsepower, two-stroke engine, and as soon as we hit second gear, ol' John was bouncing on his back tires with his hood in the air! Bucked off and dizzy, the last thing I saw of old John was his purple rear end chasing the dog up and over the ditch bank...

Beware of Cat

Most of the cats on our farm are wild. By the time the kittens appear from the hayloft able to run around, it's too late to tame them. I've cornered one here and there but backed down in a hurry when the claws came out and the kitten howled and made spitting noises reminiscent of "The Exorcist."

One particular afternoon, I heard a dreadful, blood-curdling scream from the hayloft. Investigating, I found a tiny kitten all alone with no siblings in sight. Since it was way too young to wean, I figured the mother cat was in the process of moving the litter, so I tucked the little darling in a space between some straw bales, making a note to check back the next morning.

As busy as life gets around here, I forgot about the tiny kitten until the next evening. Listening upwards toward the loft, I heard not a peep. Satisfied mama cat had come to claim the last of her litter, I headed toward the barn door.

There in the corner pen by the door was the scared-to-death kitten. Apparently, it had made its way to the ladder hole and fallen down into the cattle pen. With the little creature about two seconds away from being smashed by a thousand-pound heifer, it was Emily to the rescue in a great big hurry! Awfully stinky but cute as a bug's ear, she nestled in my coat pocket while I finished chores.

Back up to the house, the kitten was squirming and crying out for food while I didn't have a clue what to do. The image of mama cat in apron strings walking up to release me of my troubles, was a pleasant but only momentary thought.

Now the sole caretaker of a not-yet-weaned kitten, I cut the tip off a syringe and tried coaxing some milk into its mouth through that, but kitten let me know in no uncertain terms and by leaving me with a scratched-up hand that that type of feeding was for the birds.

Placing the kitten back in my pocket, I made an emergency trip to town, thinking a mini doll bottle would be about the right size for Little Stinky.

Striking out at all the toy stores and getting some pretty strange looks from the checkers as they eyed my squirming, howling coat pocket, we ended up at Petco. Holy Moly, did I find the mother lode of orphan kitten supplies there! Bottles, formula, instruction booklets—you name it, they had it. Two hours and a very expensive orphan later, I was equipped to be the kitten saver of the county. Five days later, with feedings every four hours, I was exhausted and getting post-partum syndrome.

Making it through the worst part of infancy and deciphering that the little tike was a girl, I named her Lucy. The fun part came with her first mouse toy, bringing cheers from the family and amusing entertainment as she growled and tossed the fake rodent around the house. Toilet training was a breeze in her pink heart-shaped litter box, while Lucy established herself as queen of the house.

Teenage behavior kicked in with shredded drapes and the sound of thunder running up and down the halls at night. Newspaper reading was made impossible as Lucy developed a taste for attacking the sports pages.

One evening after giving up and tossing my "who done it" reading on the floor for Little Missy to finish off, I was absolutely horrified to see two little bumps on her rear! Shaking my head and looking around at all the pink accessories and kitty toys, I found it real tough to comprehend that Lucy was a HE. I'd have to go to counseling immediately!

It took a good month of major adjustment on my part, but I decided that Lucy would keep his name and I would have a "Boy Named Sue."

Early adulthood turned Lucy into a one-woman cat. If anyone but me picked him up, his green eyes turned black and dilated, with his claws ready to shred. Lucy's growls could be heard from across the section, and if the innocent holder that now didn't dare move happened to look him in the eyes, they were toast.

We had to place a "Beware of Cat" sign on the front door after the Girl Scouts came around selling cookies. The group of ponytailed gals trotted into the house before Ed could warn them, and, to make a long story short, the boxes of cookies were used as shields and Ed was out a hundred bucks.

The UPS driver was still pretty leery of our doorstep after the goat episode but totally ignored the little sign that stated a lion lived in our home. Those big brown trucks can sure make fast tracks in reverse!

The small-animal clinic banned us and burned Lucy's records after his neutering incident; dang, how many times does a person have to emphasize the word "caution"?

Getting a call from a neighbor last week asking for advice with a batch of orphan kittens, I gave it freely. Run. Fast. Far...

Sp-rrrrrr-ing?

I know, I know, we live in Minnesota and the grand ol' "Farmer's Almanac" is the second most popular read besides the Weather Guide, but when both state it's officially spring, shouldn't it be official?

For the third time now I've packed away and then unpacked my winter Carhartts, and I'm getting a tish worried about my sanity.

Last week I left for town with all the windows in the house open and a nice green lawn. Late afternoon, I drove by the Dairy Queen and people were lined up in their late-winter/early-spring coats and boots for some nice, cool ice cream. By the time I hit our gravel road on the way home, I couldn't see the gravel, much less the road, on account of the blowing snow.

Two ducks were huddled up against the bottom of a power pole, looking very cold and bleak, and that's all I could think of after sweeping a foot of snow out the kitchen door. I couldn't just leave those ducks there to freeze, so I drove back to check on them. What I thought I was going to accomplish I don't know, but when I got close, offering a blanket and a bowl of warm water, they sure let me know they were okay. After wrapping my bloody fingers up with my stocking cap, I told those two danged ducks they could just sit there and freeze!

Waiting for spring to arrive for the third time this year, Ed was being very secretive in the shop, making sure my list of "things to do" kept me away from the building. Knowing full well what he was up to, I was very much going to enjoy my new horse feeder when it was unveiled.

Curious George that I am, I just had to peek in the shop window to make sure the width and height of the feeder weren't going to spoil the big surprise. Everything looked hunky-dory, but as I turned to leave, my stomach kind of sank as I noticed that the tracks from my boots in the snow led right up to the window. Dang, if Ed saw my tracks I would be exposed and my horse feeder would be welded right into some kind of funky lawn ornament! Very, very carefully I walked backwards in my tracks while swishing the snow back in place with my gloves.

A big old, fat robin that probably was at his wits' end in the supposed spring climate must have needed a human to vent at as he hopped around in the snow for awhile and then flew straight at my head! Walking backwards was never one of my strong suits, and down I went, flat out in the snow. I made a huge thud, the evergreen next to me let loose all its snow, and I was buried right out of sight. Hearing the door to the shop open, I had two choices: sit up out of the snow and stare at an ugly welded lawn ornament all summer long or stay buried and receive a nice shiny new horse feeder as a surprise. Calling on all the little snow angels I could muster, I held out until I heard the shop door close again.

Dreaming of the black fields weeks ago, I had Ed's water jug, lunch cooler, and coffee thermos all shined up and lined up on the kitchen counter, waiting for the morning when he would say, "See ya tonight." In farm language that means midnight and a very long and happy "Ed free" day for Emily. I don't mind lending a helping hand with livestock chores in quiet bliss, but I find it really hard to answer the phone on those days in case it may be one of those "honey, I need a pull" calls.

Bringing a late lunch out to the field is no problem either, except when the tractor is on the other end and, at five miles per hour from the half-section line, it takes thirty minutes before the nice farmer can be served up his chicken wings.

Speaking of wings, Ed was in a hurry to beat the rain one time and stopped the tractor for his lunch on the other side of a huge, deep ditch filled with water. He yelled for me to toss his lunch across the ditch, and I did just that—only, my fast-pitch softball years were well behind me and the brown bag disappeared in the middle of the water. Kicking myself for putting in an extra Little Debbie fudge brownie, I realized that, without that, the bag probably would have floated over to the other side. So much for trying to be thoughtful.

I felt kind of bad until Ed accused me of trying to starve him and all but tore his hat in half. Sure, I threw the bag, but he told me to. I stood my ground in the argument back and forth across the ditch, feeling very safe as Ed can't swim. Taking a quick mental note of my car's snack inventory, I tossed one potato chip at a time to the angry side of the ditch. Half a Hershey bar was well aimed to the very muddy edge and twenty Tic Tacs made a pretty cool trail up the bank.

It didn't matter that the tractor was already half a mile away…

Service Engine Soon

Receiving a call from a fellow horse enthusiast, I was let in on a little secret: A national trainer was driving through our state with his load of champion horses and had broken down by a small town about a hundred miles away. I checked my lottery ticket first because this opportunity was surely a once-in-a-lifetime chance to see horses in person that at any other time I would drool over in a glossy magazine.

Checking the map for the fastest available cross-country trip according to how the crow would fly, I was off in no time at all with camera and autograph pen in hand.

A bit nervous wandering into new territory by myself, I was assured by the map that there were paved roads all the way to my destination. But in a heavily wooded area with winding roads, the nice highway turned into a very narrow, almost one-lane park path. Being a perpetual optimist, I was sure the little paved road would turn back into an adult highway in no time, so I continued on with my trip to see the world champs.

Where the Amtrak train came from and where it thought it was going were two dang good questions. Probably coming from Timbuktu and en route to a city called What-cha-ma-call-it. As I looked at my watch and was getting really impatient, the train slowed down and then came to a complete stop in the middle of nowhere, blocking my way. It really ticked me off as I imagined the truck and horse trailer full of fancy steeds slipping away.

Now, I was taught some dang good manners as a child, but the mother of the little boy making faces at me through the train window was just about to get my car rammed against her reclined seat. She lucked out as the train started chugging away.

Ducks are a beautiful type of fowl, and the babies are the cutest little fur balls ever created. But when a person is in a hurry, ducks should not be crossing one at a time over a wannabe highway. Mama Duck hissed and flapped her wings at me in very disgusting "stop" sign-language as one little duckling after another waddled across the road in front of my car tires. Just how many ducks could a wood duck produce? As the seventeenth fuzzy-wuzzy chicklet crossed my path, Papa Duck brought up the rear with a quack and a wiggle of his tail, depositing an additional white stripe on the pavement.

OK, was I at the intersection of County Highway 80 or Number 3? Only the little rascal's shotgun pellets knew for sure, as the road sign had more bullet holes through it than Grandma's Dunkin' Donuts. Taking a right would possibly put me twenty miles from my destination, and a left could land me seventy miles on the other side of nowhere.

Hungry, frustrated, and afraid the champion horses would soon be on their way to California, I opted to take a right turn and munch on the candy bars in my survival kit. Digging to the very bottom, tossing out the flashlight, blanket, and moon boots, I found no candy bars — just empty wrappers. I cussed out Ed; he had driven my car the week before and had eaten my survival kit! Driving at a steady, ticked-off pace, I saw the farmsteads and then the industrial buildings getting closer together, meaning I was either approaching the correct town or somewhere in Canada.

The sound of "ding, ding, dings" along with my dashboard lighting up like a Christmas tree put my temper right through the imaginary sunroof. Stopped at the side of the road, I just sat and stared at the little message: "Service Engine Soon." Checking the gauges, I saw that the temperature wasn't up to the red yet, so I had a decision to make: save my car and never see the world's best horses in person or get out and hoof it. Hands down, off I drove with the little flashing light on my dash warning me I would soon be divorced.

The Jiffy Serve Station sign read "two miles ahead," and right beside that was the correct name of the town where I was destined to see my beauties. Figuring I could take some pictures of the horses, along with getting some quality autograph time with the trainer while my car was being fixed, I was on cloud nine.

Then suddenly, there it was: a gigantic, aluminum semi-trailer loaded with national champion horses, right in front of my very own eyes. Getting emotional, I needed to use Jiffy Serve's Jiffy John before gazing at the marvelous animals.

What happened next was beyond all devastation and fifty broken mirrors at the same time. As I came around the corner from freshening up, the horse trailer was pulling out of the driveway, never to be seen again. As I stood in total despair, the "toothless wonder"-mechanic was lucky he didn't have any after he had the nerve to say, "You thould have theen thothe horthes; they were stho boothiful."…

Away in the Manger

It was a very silent night when Ed read my Christmas list; apparently a new Featherlite Gooseneck horse trailer with air-conditioned living quarters was out of the question. Penciling the trailer in on my list had given me high hopes that at the very least a brand-new, shiny, red wheelbarrow would be in my horse barn on Christmas morning. Perfume and jewelry were out of the question; the smell of a horse in the sun and a new halter as an accessory would suit me just fine!

One year, I was the recipient of a five-foot-long piece of iron with steak knives attached to the end. Looking around for a very large cow for Christmas dinner, I was informed we would be going ice fishing. Better safe than sorry, I wore my life jacket under my parka on the miserable eight-hour "vacation" with Ed and a few others to a frozen lake with tiny houses that had no restrooms or windows.

I was granted my very own dwelling with a stinky propane heater and a five-gallon pail for a recliner. It was an immensely enjoyable outing, sitting in the dark by myself, watching the bottom of the lake through a hole while waiting for supper to swim by. A grand time for self-reflection and plotting wicked revenge, to be sure.

Remembering back to past Christmas seasons, I fondly recall the all-out brawls over the Sears toy catalogs when they arrived in the mail around the first week in December. It seems that, in a previous life, we had an entire Thanksgiving season all to ourselves without dodging tinsel and reindeer in the department store aisles.

There were no ponies listed in the Sears catalog. Dick and Jane had a dog named Spot. So did we, but they lived in town and had a pony. We lived on a farm with no pony, and I hated Dick and Jane for that!

One rather bleak Christmas morning, Dad gave Mom a most special gift: a shotgun. I remember her looking at the long box and shaking it a few times, all excited to unwrap her gift. Maybe she thought it was the newest-fangled version of a sewing machine — who knows? — but when Dad looked into the double barrels with Mom on the trigger end, he knew that Santa was not coming to his side of the tree for a very long time!

One stipulation that Mom and Dad had for a few years was that us kids were to put on a nativity play before opening our presents.

Practicing each afternoon for a week or so before Christmas Eve, we sometimes drew blood on each other before the day was over. Bandaged up and limping around, we knew "the play must go on" as the boys dreamed of Red Ryder BB guns, my sisters' hopes were for Barbie dolls, and my great vision was the Johnny West ranch set with Jane West as the heroine.

We six little angels arranged our last play to be just that — the last one — and it worked so well that we all got along great the entire practice week. With great anticipation, we asked the audience (parents and grandparents) to wait in a separate room as we prepared the stage for our grand finale while the youngest brother ushered in the props. Giggling behind the curtain and ready to put the opera to shame, we were dressed in the finest nativity clothing that Mom's old dresses would allow.

By the piano sat the dog, peeking around from behind the couch was a calf, and on top of the kitchen table stood a goat with a north star duct-taped to the top of his head. Clucking around the living room were half of the chickens from the coop, and none of the critters were following their script. Our entire cast was immediately excused from the stage, and our acting days were happily over. We did receive a sitting ovation from Grandpa as he slapped his knee and laughed at Mom who dragged the calf outside by its ears.

Grandma was very much less impressed and made a new stipulation that, from then on, all children would eat lutefisk on Christmas Eve before opening gifts. Stage fright turned into table fright for a few years…

Pigs Don't Have Necks

When I think of all the baby birds, rabbits, stray cats, and dogs (even a raccoon) that I have brought home to "save," I never figured in a million years I'd be the "saver" of a five-hundred-pound sow.

It was late fall and one of those evenings that chills you to the bone. The weatherman finally got a forecast right, saying it would start raining and then turn to sleet and snow. I was out helping Ed batten down the hatches in the barns when I saw "Big Mama" in the mud hole. Ed said, "Just leave her; she'll get out on her own." Well, that wasn't the right thing to say as I was born with the title "animal rescuer."

Coaxing with a pail of feed near the edge of the hole didn't budge Mama, nor did my little "oink, oink" noises as I pretended to be a baby piglet in distress. Threatening to turn her into pork chops went in one pretty pink ear and right out the other.

Bright ideas come from desperation as I thought of the lariat hanging in the horse barn. A family friend was a calf roper and had given me one of his old ropes to "give it a try." I did try roping from the back of a horse once, but all that was lassoed were the feet of the horse I was riding. I seemed to have a small case of "dyslexia" when it came to hanging onto the lariat, two reins, and the horse at the same time. Trying my dexterity at roping a five-gallon pail on the ground from about twenty feet away was a brilliant switch from calf roping. I prided myself on being the champion bucket-roper for miles around.

Judging Mama Sow's neck to be about the same size as the bucket, I gathered up the rope and started tossing. About that time it started to rain, a cold-to-the-bone rain, and it was getting dark. The first few tries came close; the next fifty landed on top of Mama's head, but without a neck there was no way it would drop around. By this time the rope was slick from the mud, and my gloves were lost somewhere between the fence and the mud hole.

When it started to sleet, I was so dang mad at that sow that a few swear words were blurted out that even I had never heard before. This was a battle of immense importance, and I would win or go down trying! I figured if I stood right on the edge of the hole, there might be a better shot at saving Private Mama. Losing one boot in the mud on the way in didn't stop me; losing the other one just made my day.

Ed came around the corner and turned his hat sideways after a while. I guess it was somewhat of a sight as I stood soaking wet and covered with mud from head to bare feet—yes, the goop got my socks, too. As he started to say something, I turned and gave him a look from "The Exorcist," and it didn't take him long to get far away from my little mercy mission.

I was extremely lucky about the millionth toss. It was either that or the sow was getting up on her own and the rope happened to slip down far enough that I finally had her caught. Now, trying to pull Big Mama out was a different story, what with my bare feet and no traction. My hands were frozen by this time, so I wrapped the rope around my waist and got down on my knees, pulling with everything I could muster. It was a dead-or-alive rescue at this point as I worked at blanking out the little voice in my head that was screaming that I would be the one who would not live to see another day.

Upon managing to loop the end of the rope around a post, I was finally confident both Big Mama and I would indeed wake to see sunshine in the morning.

As I stood there barefoot in freezing mud with icicles hanging from my hair, that big old sow climbed right up out of the hole. Shaking the mud off and yawning, she moseyed over for a drink of water and then went into the barn.

I was furious I wasn't acknowledged as her savior with a proper "thank you." She could have at least given my rope back!

Sometimes the weatherman does get the forecast right...

Stanley

Paperwork is the worst. The "Organizing Your Desk in One Simple Step" book is somewhere around my office. I bought it a few years ago, and after I read Chapter 1 about "only handling paperwork once," the book got buried under a paper heap, never to be seen again.

Ed doesn't do well with paper products either. All slim shavings of once-tall trees are handed over with the words "Fill this out or file it, would ya?"

Smack dab on the middle of my desk yesterday was a very important-looking government envelope sporting a sticky-note from Ed that read, "These livestock forms need to be filled out and mailed within thirty days." Thirty days is a very long time; he should never have given me that much leeway. As a result, the envelope was placed on the "to do" pile as we were heading to town for supplies.

Moseying around the hardware store, I couldn't help but notice that Ed had been standing in one spot in aisle four for a very long time. Knowing full-well this was his "I want it" stance, I avoided aisle four until the lights dimmed and management announced the store would be closing soon.

It was the Stanley Thermos aisle, and Ed was holding one like a newborn, telling me his father and his father's father had owned indestructible Stanleys that kept their grits and coffee warm for almost a century. Then, playing the trump card, Ed stated that, just the other day, his cousin Carl had poured a steaming cup of coffee for himself from his bright green Stanley in the late afternoon while Ed's inadequate thermos poured the iced-tea variety.

OK, OK, but just keep in mind that the rather large and sparkly item in aisle nine would be coming home with Emily on the next trip to town.

Ed was in such a hurry to try out his new Stanley that he left the engine running and the pickup door wide open when we arrived home. Hot coffee was poured into the thermos while he sat at the kitchen table, waiting the required time to "test the waters." Figuring I would get at the important paperwork left on my desk before it disappeared into another pile, I was delighted to find multiple-choice questions on the form. Who can go wrong with multiple choice?

"Defect, defect, defect," Ed was mumbling as he walked into my office, holding Stanley out in front of him like a broken Christmas present. The poor guy's dream of owning a family heirloom went right down the drain with the lukewarm liquid it produced. Not to worry, Ed; I would return Stanley the next day for another model and, killing two birds with one stone, the large, shiny trinket from aisle nine could be hauled home at the same time.

After I handed the replacement model over to him the next evening, Ed was again thrilled to "test the waters" for steaming hot coffee as I put my "multiple choice" face on and, for a second time, tried to fill out the important livestock forms.

Holy Hannah! — was there ever a spiel coming from the kitchen a while later, with an airborne stainless steel lid flying by my office door.

I felt kind of sorry for the Stanley Thermos associate on the other end of the phone the next morning, but by the time all was said and done, Ed had a big smile on his face, saying the company was sending out a new thermos and to toss the old one away. Dang, I sure wished I could do that with the laundry!

Setting the important forms aside to read horse magazines, I figured I had ten days yet to postmark the envelope, so I could wait while my multiple-choice wisdom was replenished.

A few days later, I placed the envelope containing a "replacement seal" on the kitchen table. I decided it would be safer to be in the horse barn for a few hours rather than in the house when Ed came home to "test the waters" and discovered that only *part* of a thermos had been sent.

Stanley associate number two was very apologetic and assured Ed he would receive a *complete* new thermos within seven days. I marked the calendar, as day seven was also when the important papers needed to be postmarked.

The post office closed at 4:30 and I had all day to fill out the forms and get them mailed. The UPS truck pulled in just as Ed was driving out, so he got a quick chance to feel and "test the waters" of Stanley number three. More excited than when he had received a Red Rider BB gun on his thirteenth birthday, Ed waltzed into my office with two empty cups, defective Stanley number two, and newest model number three, poured from both and set them on my desk. Examining the hot steam rising from one cup and the drab cool liquid in the other, Ed was thrilled to death as he ran out the door to pour a cup of coffee in front of Cousin Carl.

I didn't dare say a word as the cups left big smeared smudges and illegible print on the very-important-paperwork forms.

Those Stanley people were real kind; perhaps they could give me a nice multiple-choice job and a relocation to a place far, far away…

Daze n Nights

Talking to my friend Brandy about the thirteen-inch color TV I had in my horse barn and how clear it came in was a mistake as Ed rounded the corner, catching the tail end of the conversation, and was down to the barn in a jiffy pilfering my outside entertainment. I guess I agreed part-ways to being ripped off, but only for the time it took to finish combining the corn.

With a very wet fall, it was closing in on November, and by now the crops are usually in, the ground worked, machinery cleaned up and under cover, and Uncle Curt has hibernated for the winter. Do not—I repeat, do not—try to make small talk or a funny until the last corn cob is in the elevator. It may get you a space on the obituary page or, worse yet, a seat in the number-two combine that the fart smell will never diminish from after last year's field lunch of egg salad sandwiches and a side order of hard-boiled eggs in the same meal.

Ed lost the coin flip and received the night watch to run the grain dryer this year. Having never worked past midnight or before four in the morning, this was a little bitty change in habit for both of us. Packing up his supplies after dark, my TV, wrapped in a towel so it wouldn't get scratched, was the first item placed in the truck. "Hey, Ed, it's full of fly crap and horse poop; I think it'll be OK." Next was his Stanley Thermos filled to the brim with coffee. I had a hard time brewing coffee in the evening, and the coffeemaker blew a fuse for the same reason. Sandwiches, Little Debbie's fudge brownies, and a few hard-boiled eggs (eeek!) rounded out his lunch box.

"See ya later" was followed by "please bring me supper before you go to bed." Now my mind was in major confusion and I wasn't sure if I should bring him pancakes or hotdish. According to the time zone, the meal I brought him should be his lunch that was already packed, and supper should be sometime after sunrise.

After delivering breakfast / lunch / supper or whatever Ed wanted to call it, I was asked to call him if I woke up during the night, to make sure he was awake and the elevator hadn't burnt down. Hmmm. Crap, didn't he realize that what he had just said immediately inserted the mothering instinct into my mind? One o'clock—you awake? Yep, OK. Two o'clock—you awake? Yep, OK. Three o'clock—the TV isn't coming in clear; can I borrow your digital receiver from the kitchen television tomorrow night? Lack of sleep makes you say silly things, but I still don't remember agreeing to that one, and with my luck, the dang thing would actually work surrounded by four steel walls. At four o'clock, Ed's got everything under control with the corn drying and he wants to visit! That's too bad that the number-five bin plugged up. I'm sorry to hear you had to eat your hotdish with the lid; I'll remember to pack a fork tomorrow night. No, I haven't heard the forecast lately. Yes, I do think we should sell that old sow and you along with it…. Ed?

Wondering what I would do if he didn't answer the phone, I lay awake for an hour thinking of disastrous grain-dryer fires and crippled Eds falling off the elevator in the middle of the night. It was wicked cold and would be a bit of a drive in a very chilly car. Ed, you awake? Oh, excuse me, I didn't mean to interrupt your CBS morning show!

When my alarm went off, I answered the phone, and when the phone rang, I shut off the alarm. You awake? Yes, Ed, I'm awake.

Flipping the covers in place was a breeze; that was it, bed made! It was so easy, I did it again! Coffee! Tons and tons of coffee, all to myself with no dribbles on the counter. Shower—all the hot water I ever wanted and then some. It was so dang nice, I took two!

With the night's check-up calls catching up to me, I started to slow down by the time Ed arrived home, and as he was walking in the door and I out, we simultaneously said to each other, "You look like crap." Then he said in passing, "If you think of it later, call and wake me up…"

Union Rules

Growing up, the six of us kids each had our list of chores posted for the week, usually classified between "boys' jobs" and "girls' jobs."

Paydays were intensely competitive as any overtime or volunteer work was rewarded with an extra nickel or two. The $1-a-week base was top take-home pay for any countryside kid at the time, and salary increases were not on the bargaining table as we valued both our health and our lives.

At the time, overwork and underpayments were never in our thoughts as a whole dollar could purchase a sizeable hundred-piece bag of penny candy.

On a sunny Saturday while sifting through our workers' compensation of jaw breakers and bubble gum, older brother brought up the subject of job diversity and his two co-workers chimed in with a bashing to us girls that our meek and mild labor didn't qualify for equal pay. The screaming match that followed promptly transferred us all by the ears to the chief executive officer's milking room with a scolding and reversal of job duties for the following seven days.

We tossed our ponytails at the boys as we walked away, knowing full-well we could execute their chores faster and far more efficiently than they ever could. That brought sneers of sissy words and attempted high-heeled walking to our turned backs.

Under the "girls'" column of chores Monday morning was listed grinding feed for the pigs and feeding the cows. Immediately taking notes to bring it to the CEO's attention that we were being discriminated against, our thoughts turned to the boys and their duties in the kitchen, and we happily shoveled corn into the grinder, asking each pig how they would like their prepared meal—over-easy, with catsup, or well-done and crunchy.

By mid-morning, little sister was propped against the tractor tire, complaining of the blisters on her hands, and I was screaming at big sister to stop petting the dog and grab a shovel. I was promptly the target of a scoop full of corn over my head that started a little Boston Tea Party event that was quickly brought to an end by the CEO's pickup driving in the yard.

Getting our grip and joining forces again, at lunch time we skipped to the house, eagerly anticipating the boys' service of food and reminding each other to drop crumbs on the floor after spilling our milk glasses.

One look at the kitchen table brought tears and rebellious jealousy to our little work force of three. A nice, neat stack of sandwich meat and bread was centered on the kitchen table with condiments and utensils precisely arranged in the shape of a star. Walking past to wash our hands, we received pure gratification as little brother was spotted by the counter on his hands and knees, mopping up flour with a damp rag. Not needing to drop or spill a thing, we merrily ate our lunch as big brother used a claw hammer to un-stick his shoes from the linoleum floor before Mom came home. Neatly penciling our initials into the homemade glue as we walked out the door, we dodged flour bombs halfway across the yard as evil eyes were cast and the war was on.

It was near dark before the feed grinding was done, and we gladly changed job locations to feed the cows. Pitching hay over the fence was the easy part; the difficult task was using a one-tine pitchfork. Apparently, the boys had sabotaged our work station by removing all but one of the tines and were spying on us from around the corner and laughing up a storm.

With bets placed between our little work assembly the next morning as we pretended to move a rock pile, little sister was the first-place winner as, right about 9 a.m., the boys started running out of the house gagging and rolling around in the grass. Our strategic planning worked to a T and high fives were cast as the rotten goose eggs planted in the jean pockets exploded one at a time and right on schedule as the washer started agitating and the lid was lifted by all three boys at once to find the source of the racket.

Waking up the next morning, all three of us girls were covered in a terrible itchy rash and cursed big brother as he leaned against the washing machine, twirling an empty bottle of bleach.

While fixing boards on the cow fence, the lovely noise of an oven door blowing off brought smiles to our pony-tailed work force. Big sister's bright idea of replacing cooking oil with gasoline and masking the smell with vanilla was the best!

Cute, cute, cute… When feeding the pigs, we noticed that the biggest three had our names spray-painted on their sides.

The boys received a double deduction in pay when the garden was weeded and the only plants left standing were the weeds. It remains an unsolved mystery as to how the little seed packages that marked the rows were mixed around.

Toward the end of the week, we should have known it was a bad idea for all three of us to enter a grain bin at the same time to clean it out, as work detail number two was outside hanging laundry on the clothesline and sheets tied end to end around the bin made a very strong hold on the door.

Vacuum cleaners make a bigger mess than the Dust Bowl in the '30s when there's a hole cut in the bag. It was Ladies' Circle day at our house, and the spare bags had mysteriously disappeared. Mom made all six of us clean up the mess, one dust bunny at a time, and promptly overrode the CEO's chore reversal arrangement while throwing up her hands as the six of us wrote secret notes to each other in the dust on the furniture…

Complicated Competition

Horse shows and rodeos are great events. Sometimes the weather is a little annoying or the drive to the arena a little long, but once you get there it's all horse bliss!

One of the biggest mistakes I ever made was agreeing to ride a neighbor's horse in a fifty-mile endurance ride through a national forest in chilly October. Vince was the god of horse knowledge in our small community, and when he asked me (a mere teenager) to ride his lovely mare Lady in a cross-country race, I agreed hands-down before hindsight caught up to me.

Receiving the training details, I decided it was the most fun a girl could ever have on a horse as the conditioning route passed a McDonald's and the mileage worked out perfectly to ride through the drive-up for an after-school snack.

With both Lady and me in tiptop shape, her with a fresh set of shoes and me sporting a shiny new pair of boots, we were ready to conquer the sixty other participants. Eyeing them up the night before was an important thing to do. I felt pretty smug in my bell-bottom jeans and braided hair. As I passed nerd after nerd polishing their tack, I daydreamed about which wall I would hang my blue ribbon on.

Then, I froze in place and felt like a black sheep as I noticed that every saddle on the grounds was of English construction while I had come to the competition with my heavy old saddle from the west. Calling Mom in a panic, I begged her to scavenge the neighborhood and call in all favors to borrow an English saddle and possibly deliver it to the event.

With a big number 48 painted on Lady's rump the next morning, we gathered with all the contestants in a grassy area, ready to rock and roll through the next fifty miles.

The officials let groups of five at a time out on the trail, and being number 48, it was all I could do to hold Lady back as she saw 47 horses trot off into the wilderness without her. By the time it was our turn to start, Lady was hopping on her hind legs and I was holding onto her mane for dear life, as those dang English saddles have no horn!

I saw mile marker five through a streak of tears as we galloped, then Lady slowed down to a steady trot around marker ten. Not used to posting in an English saddle, by mile marker fifteen I couldn't feel my legs. I remember praying to go back in time and suck up to the nerds to keep my comfortable western saddle, and at the same time kicked myself for agreeing to such an idiotic competition at all.

Rider number 16 came up behind me at a fast posting trot, and as I politely tried a little conversation, I was snubbed as the gal disappeared into the forest. Wondering if it was the braids or the bell-bottoms that offended her, I decided it might be the way I was sitting on my horse (sideways). No longer able to post in the teeny tiny English saddle, it was natural to find the most comfortable position I could!

I promised myself I'd let the air out of number 16's tires if I ever made it back to camp, and Lady and I treaded on.

Rounding a corner, to my amazement there was a clearing filled with horses, people, and food! I had reached the halfway point and was allowed a short break while Lady was checked for soundness and given a drink of water.

An hour later, passing mile marker 35, I realized that eating four sandwiches and downing three cans of Coke was probably not a good idea back at the halfway point. Talk about leaving breadcrumbs in the forest, Hansel and Gretel would have been proud!

Lady had gotten her second wind at marker 40 while I was just hanging on for the ride, unable to feel anything from the waist down. As we approached a meadow with a lonely tree in the middle of it, the next occurrence resembled walking in a football field while not looking where you were going and running smack dab into the goal post. I had bark implanted into my forehead and landed flat on the ground. While trying to mount with no feeling in my legs or now my head, I contemplated how many rolls of toilet paper it would take to cover Vince's house.

I'd been heading south before the little "Paul Bunyan incident," but now I was completely turned around. The sun was no help as it was directly overhead. I was flipping a twig on the direction to ride, but a flock of geese saved the day as they flew over on their way to a warmer climate.

Following the geese, I felt sure Lady and I would finish in the top five and I would be given a homecoming parade along with the city key.

Informing the two gals cantering toward me that they were going in the wrong direction, I received peculiar stares as they passed. Picking up the pace, I could see the final mile marker dead ahead with my victory dance to follow.

Standing in front of mile marker number forty, I silently hoped the flock of geese kept right on flying to the North Pole and froze...

Creepy Crawlers

Being born and raised on a farm and then marrying a farmer, I've gotten used to about everything there is except bugs. I HATE BUGS!

While growing up, I don't seem to remember the wave after wave of different "creepy crawlers" we have nowadays. It seems like one group settles down and you can walk outside without getting bombarded, and the next day it starts all over again with a hatch of something else.

The common fly is easy; they don't bite or attack unless provoked. Did you know they take off backwards? Swat a tish behind one and it's a squashed fly every time.

The biting-fly variety is the worst. No human or animal is safe from their hungry little jaws; they can chew you up right through a thick pair of Wrangler jeans and drive a herd of buffalo insane in a matter of minutes.

Have you ever rolled your car after a grasshopper jumped in through the open window, landing on your neck?

I remember when a big fat bumblebee chased Grandpa into a pen of bulls. I guess he felt safer in there than on the outside with the quarter-ounce bee's brothers and sisters.

No-See-'Ems are just that: you can't see the little creeps until they've taken a bite out of you. Talk about driving a person off the deep end! At least the biting flies can be spotted before you turn into an incredible edible.

Crickets are harmless, until one sneaks into the house and starts its miserable chirping serenade. Locating one is like playing "red light, green light." If you get close, it stops making noise; back away and it'll start driving you nuts again.

What's with the new breed of fat little black beetles that have built-in sonar, can fly, and dive-bomb innocent passersby?

We won't even touch on the subject of Asian beetles; that's another whole story.

These are just a few I have a little problem with off the top of my list of creepy crawlers, but whoever is responsible for bringing the wood tick to the North American continent should have been hanged from the nearest tree!

This little scoundrel gives me the heebie-jeebies for a week if I even hear the word, much less see or feel one crawling on me.

A few years back, my friend Brandy asked me along to look at a horse she was thinking of buying. To get a close look at the fine steed, we had to walk quite a ways into his pasture. After catching up to him and admiring him, I felt the first "crawl" on my leg. Then the second, and third... I turned into a crazy woman, making Brandy pick the ticks off me as I jumped around thinking I could shake them off.

While I stood on top of a fence post, Brandy had to drive into the pasture to pick me up as there was NO way I was walking back through the long grass to the pickup — never mind that the farmer working in the next field had stopped his tractor and was staring, probably thinking he should call the people in white coats to bring a straitjacket.

Taco John's is always an automatic stop for Brandy and me on our way home from any adventure, and I was satisfied that all the ticks had been left behind with the herd of horses. At the drive-through, I reached for my bag of lunch and, crawling right on the T for "Taco" and heading straight toward the J for "John's" on the outside of the bag, was a creepy-crawling wood tick!

How the evil little bugger hopped on the bag so fast and where it came from I don't know, but the large Pepsi in one hand and the bag of tacos in the other both went flying back past Brandy and into the cashier's window. Brandy had seen it coming and ducked, but the cashier with soda and lettuce all over his shirt asked in a steady voice, "Miss, was there a problem with your meal?"

Neither one of us would admit to the young man that a little bug could make a grown woman go so far off the deep end, and Brandy never would tell me what she whispered back to him. But looking in the rear view mirror as we drove off sure made me feel better as the cashier was diving out headfirst right through the little window to escape his new friend...

Taken for a Ride

And here I thought the straw was finished / done / over for the year. Think again, Emily; life on the farm can never be that easy!

Not an hour after I had hosed down our afternoon helpers, shaken the straw out of their boots, and hauled them back to the family reunion Ed says, "Come on, Emily, I need your help for a little bit longer." Oh, crap, that "little bit" makes me want to run for the hills every time.

I listened to Mom when she said, "Marry for love, not for money," but I wish I would have listened a little closer when she advised not to marry a farmer.

The Donahue trailer was hooked up to a tractor and conveniently hidden around the corner of the barn. There's a word for what my thoughts were, but "Spelling and Grammar Check" won't let me type it.

So, here sits this ten-by-thirty-five-foot trailer with a skid steer sitting directly in the middle. As I'm standing there looking around for places to hide, Ed drives by in the pickup, pulling another trailer, and says, "Follow me."

Now, it's been a few years or longer since I graduated from field work to making tasty sack lunches, and my knees buckled when I climbed the steps up into the John Deere. The seat looked comfortable and the throttle was in the right place, but my mind blew up when I looked at the gears. There wasn't just one shifter, but two, and the numbers beside them counted to twenty-nine!

Four shifts, reverse, and road gear made up my last tractor skills, and this jumbled mess just didn't compute. Good thing for cell phones and hat salesmen as Ed screeched back to the farm for a quick gear-direction lesson.

I flunked, totally. There was no way I was going to get that tractor down the road and into the field if I had to figure out both columns, so we decided on one low gear that would get me there slow, but get me there. Thinking back here, why was *I* driving the tractor instead of the simple, five-speed pickup? Hmmmm.

The last thing Ed said as I held the clutch in was, "Easy on the corners; the skid steer's a little tippy and the hitch on the trailer is about ready to fall off." Talk about an outstanding diet plan; three pounds of sweat immediately let loose.

All-righty then, we got to live another day as the skid steer, trailer, and I made it to the field in one piece. I won't elaborate on the corners or steep field-road approach. Let's just say the extended diet plan was working top-notch.

It wasn't even an option for me to unload the skid steer; Ed knew that. I couldn't find the neutral gear to put the dang tractor at ease, so why was he just sitting in the pickup staring at me?

It took awhile, but the plan took shape as I drove the tractor down the rows of straw and Ed zoomed around with the skid steer. The best invention anyone ever thought of was to weld together a contraption to pull behind the baler that left neat packs of eight bales so the pick-er-upper thing on the skid steer could grab 'em and stack 'em with ease. Geez, used to be we had to run beside the trailer and stack by hand — isn't technology splendid?!

It was getting dark and hard to see the points and nods for directions between the rows. By this time, I really wanted to give Ed a direction with one of my center fingers but figured he wouldn't see it anyway. As I drove the tractor right over the top of one of the eight-packs of straw and obliterated it, there was enough light left to see the skid steer zipping around in a hissy-fit circle.

The tractor cab heater had felt real good earlier, but now we had a little problem: It was sweltering and I didn't have a clue which knob controlled the heat. Sure as heck, I would turn the wrong one and blow up both the tractor and myself. Also, I could stop with the clutch in, but couldn't take my foot off as the neutral gear was hidden somewhere amongst the twenty-nine.

But the worst was yet to come as kind radio announcer number one was replaced by nighttime comic number two. Of course, the volume knob was somewhere in the vicinity of the ceiling, but the "Don't touch or it will blow up" rule kept my hands on the steering wheel; I was forced to listen to his very un-funny ramblings about a broken dishwasher and a fumbling repairman. Blanking out his jibber-jabber, I was surviving until he decided to play us cranky listeners a nice country jingle.

No, no, no, not that song!! "Big Green Tractor" made my foot slip off the clutch, causing the tractor to lurch forward, breaking the hitch off the trailer and scattering straw bales from here to kingdom come. I was really glad it was dark; this time I could only hear the skid steer going around and around in circles…

Moose Among Us

Moose can't hide very well. The bigger they are, the more commotion they cause around the county. Word spreads faster than little old ladies' gossip. "Did you see the moose?" "Did you see the huge moose?" "Did you see the biggest moose that's ever been around here?" All the while, it's the same small yearling trotting around from field to field.

My first close encounter with a moose happened in a cornfield while I was driving truck during harvest. At the end of a ten-hour day of repeating the same route over and over with tall corn on each side of the truck, I was startled to see the moose amble around the corner and stop directly in the middle of the field road. With both feet jammed on the brake pedal and after the corn stopped pouring over the front of the windshield, I found myself looking directly into the eyes of the monstrous moose. Pretty naïve about moose habits, I failed to recognize that a stomp of the hoof and a snort meant my grain truck was about to be removed from his walkway. As the moose's antlers caught the front bumper to obliterate the truck and tip me out for stomping, reverse gear was found in a hurry and the truck was backed through the corn field next to the nearest combine for safety.

Shunned by all the field operators for wrecking a whole lot of corn, I was placed on indefinite lunch-hauling leave, incredulous that no one believed my moose-attack story.

A few years later, my good friend Brandy and I were off on one of our adventures when a gangly yearling moose trotted across the highway a ways in front of us. Being a western North Dakota native, Brandy had never seen a moose up close and was all agog about the "camel" that must have escaped from a Minnesota zoo.

Seeing moose tracks on a gravel road, I've always wondered how their sonar works. Resembling Uncle Curt's tracks from his pickup to the house after a late night at the pub, the moose's footprints wander from one side of the road to the other for miles, making their walking distance twice as far as it should have been. Maybe their antlers get to leaning one way and then the other while the body follows?

One time, a big old cow moose took up residence in the corner of the horse pasture, dismantling a three-board fence like it was toothpicks. It took about a week to round up the horses after she moseyed over to "greet" them.

Another time, a young bull moose walked right into our yard as I was hauling groceries into the house. Disappointed I was the only one home, I just had to take a few snapshots of the "National Geographic" moment. Grabbing the camera, I followed behind the visitor as he wandered around the farm, tasting flowers and evergreens. Waiting to get some close-up shots, I snuck up within a few feet of the handsome young moose. Well, my rather large photography subject turned around and gave me a look like I was the paparazzi stalking him! I didn't dare move, and he just stood there staring at me while chewing up a mouthful of my prize peony bush. Why didn't I think of the "zoom" lens a few minutes ago?

"Farm Woman Trampled by Moose" would be the headline of tomorrow's paper, and there would be a photo of me all wrapped up in bandages, lying in a hospital bed. Mr. Moose slowly put his head down and let out a snort, then started pawing the ground. This was NOT a "Kodak Moment" and brought back memories of a corn field and a truck! Either way I looked at it, I was a dead woman, so I took off running for the nearby garage with the moose close on my heels. How many times had I told the family to lock the garage door? Did they listen to me? No, only on the day I would be chased down and killed by a moose!

Mr. Moose gave up after two or three trips around the garage. He just stopped and swished his tail while walking away like nothing had happened. Didn't he realize I would now have "Moose Phobia" and would need counseling? I would see moose tracks on the gravel road and crash my car! I would watch reruns of "Northern Exposure" and cry! My kids would never, ever be allowed to watch "Rocky and Bullwinkle!"

My family wouldn't believe a word when I told them of my harrowing experience, but the pictures would sure show them! Yep, you bet—a poetic shot of the peony bush, a portrait of long grass, a beautiful skyline with fluffy clouds, and the last one of a perfectly framed garage door…

.

Going, Going, Gone

Monday morning at ten, an equine shipping company is going to drive into our yard with a gigantic aluminum trailer to pick up a colt and deliver him halfway across the country to his new home.

My, oh my, we've come a long ways from driving to the local horse sale a few miles away, purchasing our steeds, and then hauling them home in the backs of our pickups in a rusted old stock rack.

The new age of computers has let us shop, buy, and have a horse delivered to our door in less time than it used to take to drive to the County Fair!

My very first experience of listing and selling a horse on the most wonderful World Wide Web was quite interesting. The instructions were quite simple and listed three easy steps: write a description, load the photo, and pay by credit card. Poof! — your horse would be viewed instantly by millions of savvy horse shoppers, and in no time at all you would be swamped by inquiries and purchase orders. Okey-dokey, let's get started then.

First of all, to navigate the horse-selling site was way beyond science fiction to me. Writing the description at step number one was easy, until the error message said it was too long and my horse would be deleted. Too long, my rump; this was a nice horse and I wanted to brag all about him. Nope, this time it was a "fatal error" and the site was going to report me for suspicious behavior. Ohhh, so sorry; I sure didn't want to be arrested for talking too much about my horse now, did I?

Step two: Load the photo. Excuse me? Loading a horse I could do, but photo loading was not one of my best suits. The little "help" button popped up, along with a lengthy conversation with a nice gal in Timbuktu-land, and three hours later I had a darling picture of my horse right in the little box where it was supposed to be.

Step three: Pay by credit card. This was scary as all my elders and all the TV commercials said don't ever place your personal information on the Internet. How silly — just look at all these people that have entrusted this wonderful horse-selling site with their credit card information. The little "help" button assured me the site was secure, so I went ahead and typed in the numbers, looking over my shoulder the whole time for the imaginary hacker to grab the card out of my hand and charge a boob job.

Done; my horse was ready to be purchased by thousands of onlookers fighting tooth and nail for him. I clicked on and off the site, admiring my animal while comparing him to the others listed, and waited for inquiries. Holy cow, the counter said five people had already viewed my advertisement! Oops! — silly you, Emily, that would be the five times that you yourself viewed the ad.

The next few days did bring interested inquiries to my e-mail box, along with some really strange questions: "How high is this horse?" That would be listed in the description, unless you would like to hear about the neighbor kid. "Does your horse jump?" Yep, he jumps right over the fence when he wants some greener grass. "Does your horse have all his shots?" Yaaa, I suppose you could shoot a rabbit off him, but stay away from the coyotes; he'll dump you in the dirt faster than you can count the stars.

One lady finally called on the phone from way down south and asked if it would be a problem to take some outdoor pictures the next day and e-mail them to her. Hmmm, it was 25 below with a 30-mph north wind. Yep, big problem!

The next serious caller was a gentleman living on the East Coast. He commented sarcastically on my accent, and I told him my horse would probably not like living anywhere east of the Mississippi and asked if I could send him some complimentary lutefisk from the Dakota Territories.

Each evening I would hurry in to the house to check for phone messages and e-mails inquiring about my magnificent horse offering. This was just the coolest way anyone had ever thought of to sell a horse!

When I was visiting with our neighbor about my Internet sales experience, she asked about the horse, we got to chatting, and guess who bought him?

The horse lived happily ever after, five miles away...

Tomfoolery

I had been getting chores done early as Ed and I had plans to go out to supper. There was about an hour of daylight left when I heard the blood-curdling screams of the lost kitten in the shelterbelt. By the sounds of it, the poor little thing couldn't have been more than a few weeks old, and as I made mental notes of all orphan kitten supplies in the house, Ed gave me the "OK, go; I'll eat hot dogs for supper" look.

In my mind, I had already named the kitten Charlie, and when I found him, he would be black with four white paws and sport the cutest pink nose, along with a white tip on his tail.

Walking through the tall grass on the edge of the trees was hair-raising, as I knew there would be creepy crawlers I couldn't see ready to eat me alive. But Charlie was lost, hungry, and really making a fuss. Furious that the mother cat couldn't come and rescue her own kitten, I tripped over a log and banged my knee up pretty dang good. Limping into the trees, I could tell Charlie was just ahead as the frantic little meows were getting louder.

A thicket of bramble burrs was a tough obstacle to get through, and a cotton T-shirt didn't help any. I looked and felt like Bigfoot in the forest on a very bad hair day.

Hearing Charlie just on the other side of a big patch of burning weed, I did what any kitten saver would do—put my arms up and treaded through. "Ouch" and a few whispered swear words so the young kitten wouldn't hear and get a complex right off the bat; "Don't worry, Charlie, I'm coming to the rescue!" Dang, for the young age of this fellow he could scamper pretty fast, but I figured he was just afraid of me and would soon come to his senses that I was only there to help.

Now at a corner of the farm I'd never been to before, deep in the trees, the heebie-jeebies set in. It was close to dark and beside a fallen tree was an old, old pitchfork—just stuck in the ground as if someone had just been there ahead of me and was lurking around ready to pounce.

Charlie's screams brought me back to reality before I could imagine any other bogeymen on the prowl. "Here, kitty, kitty… whether you like it or not, you're going to be rescued and adopted by a nice little old lady and served warm milk every night."

I didn't want to use my trusty Mini Mag flashlight as it might scare Charlie further, but I had no choice as it was about pitch dark. About that time, Charlie's scream changed, or rather, he was higher up off the ground.

Dang, he had crawled up a tree, and I sure didn't have a choice but to go up after him.

"Easy, Charlie, don't be afraid; we'll soon be in a nice warm house all cozy and safe."

Half-ways up the mighty oak, I got to thinking that if this kitten could climb trees, maybe he was a bit older than I had figured and just might be OK on his own. Hanging on with both arms around the tree trunk, I searched the branches, clenching the Mini Mag in my mouth. No kitten could be spotlighted, but his frantic cries kept me climbing.

What the Sam Heck? Charlie was now frantically, screaming from the next tree over! How could a teeny-weenie, lost and lonely kitten jump 10 feet from one tree to the next? As the flashlight fell to the ground, I heard Charlie's cries jump to the next tree and then the next. Perplexed as all get-out, slithering halfway and falling the rest, I made a semi-soft landing right on top of an old, rusted barbed-wire fence.

They wouldn't let me into the clinic until I had picked all the burs off. Soon I was dressed pretty in pink calamine lotion and got a tetanus shot that hurt like a son of a gun. The doctor asked the usual questions but repeated twice the ones on home safety.

In the lounge waiting for the X-Ray results on my knee, I picked up and flipped through a bird magazine titled "Bird Bazaar." To my utter astonishment, there in the centerfold was a picture of Charlie! It wasn't the photo that gave him away; it was the description of his rather unusual chatter: "like a kitten in distress," a member of the Cuckoo Bird family.

"Dear Audubon Society…"

Los Angeles Visits the Farm

My side of the family hadn't had a reunion in twenty-some years. This was the BIG ONE; everyone from near and far was coming to eat, drink, and be merry. If any lopsided relative happened to recognize a family member or distant cousin, all the better.

Uncle Harry and Aunt Helen were to be our house guests for the duration of the festivities. They chose Ed and me to room with as they had never been to a (real) farm before and thought it would be a gas.

Our company arrived off the plane wearing matching plaid shirts, straw hats, and cowboy boots. Aunt Helen sported a huge straw purse to complete her get-up. OK, we could deal with this; no one knew us at the airport. "Welcome to the Dakota Territories!" were Ed's welcoming words to our guests, and his last until we got home.

The first thing Aunt Helen wanted to see was a baby pig, but two steps into the barn her gag reflex kicked in. Reaching into her big straw bag, she pulled out a bottle of "Safari by Ralph Lauren" perfume and spritzed it in the air around her while walking down the aisle. The barn started smelling like the women's accessories end of JC Penney's, and Aunt Helen resembled a priest sprinkling holy water.

After holding, cuddling, and cooing to baby pigs, and fifty-some smiling photos later, we were off to the next barn. I was a little nervous about what Aunt Helen would say when I served up a platter of pork chops for supper.

The cow barn was Uncle Harry's dream. "I've always wanted to milk a cow," he stated as we walked in with Aunt Helen and her fragrance following. I tried to explain to Uncle Harry that we didn't milk cows here; we just fed our steers and hauled them to market. "What kind of cows steer things?" he asked, and I gave Ed the "It's your turn to explain" look. Ohh boy, this was going to be a long day!

As we entered the horse barn, a group of kittens gathered around Aunt Helen looking for table scraps, and she was immediately in seventh heaven while easing her grip on the Ralph Lauren bottle. Each kitten received a proper name, brushing, and a pedicure. I wasn't sure and didn't get a head count, but I think she stuffed a couple of kittens in her bag. Uncle Harry wanted to ride a horse. As I saddled up trusty Old Grey, he reached for Aunt Helen's big straw purse for a snack.

"Have you ridden a horse before, Uncle Harry?"

"Oh no, but I've seen plenty of westerns on TV; I'll be just fine."

"OK, you get on and I'll lead you around for a bit till you get the hang of it."

It took a while but Uncle Harry made it up on top of the horse and then just slowly kept going over and off the other side, splattering to the ground. Sitting up, he yelled to Aunt Helen, "HELEN, I've been bucked off! Isn't it wonderful?" The old horse, having never taken a step, looked around at Harry and yawned. I got the giggles and had to excuse myself for a while to re-group while Ed just stood there and swallowed his snoose.

Visiting the chickens was hopeless. Aunt Helen assigned each hen a title along with a surname while Uncle Harry made the mistake of trying to pet a rooster. Aunt Helen used her perfume spray like a mad woman, fending off the rooster in no time at all.

A tractor ride was the next adventure. Ed took our guests down the road a ways and, over the engine noise, I could hear Aunt Helen singing the "Green Acres" lyrics. Uncle Harry chimed in with "Country Highway," and I received the silent treatment from Ed the rest of the night.

Before supper, I asked our company if they would trot out to the garden and pick some carrots and lettuce for a nice salad. Busy in the kitchen with my back to them as they went out the door, I heard the dog barking hysterically. In the garden were my two guests, dressed from head to toe in mosquito netting and hip waders, using spades to dig up the lettuce! Easy, Emily, we can plant more.

The reunion went off without a hitch, and my favorite aunt and uncle returned to California a few days later. Downtown L.A. will never be the same...

Westward Ho!

Not trusting the standard photos or videos, I got the silly notion in my head to inspect in person the mare that jumped right out of the advertisement saying, "Buy me!"

Traveling is not one of my strong suits, and this little trip required an above-the-ground, over-the-mountains, twelve-hundred-mile airplane ride.

Sick to my stomach for a week in advance, I checked the weather forecast daily for overabundance of wind the day of my flight. Preparing to "jump ship" if there was one little wiggle of turbulence in the air, I stashed zip-lock baggies of Dramamine and Alka-Seltzer in my purse.

Not having flown for many, many years, the last plane I had boarded was parked on a runway and we just drove up to it in the pickup, hopping aboard while the captain greeted each passenger with a "Howdy doody" and a bag of donuts.

"Overwhelming" would be a short description of the pre-flight destination. Badge-wearing officials lurked in every corner equipped with wands and guns, escorting us travelers through a maze of ropes and riggings. The black tent in the corner looked just like the lopsided Boy Scout version we had in the backyard as youngsters, and I was humbled a bit until I overheard an official on the inside directing a fellow to drop his drawers.

When the gum-smacking clerk asked me to place my shoes in the tote on the conveyer belt, I got a bit suspicious but complied. "Ma'am, your shoes please." Shrugging and looking at the lady behind me, I questioned the sanity of all airport personnel and pointed to my boots, properly placed in the correct container. "Your shoes, please" was repeated for the third time by the principal of the lunch line as she made a threatening glance toward the black tent. Getting dressed in the dark that morning so Ed could continue on with his beauty sleep, I was a little embarrassed when pointing first to my black sock and then to the blue un-matched mate to show Miss Fussy that, yes indeed, I had handed over my footwear for proper inspection.

Dang, I was wearing earrings and lipstick; was there a dress code in this particular airport that a girl couldn't wear boots?

For the life of me, I couldn't figure out how a little bitty seat cushion would save me from drowning, especially when there was only one five-gallon lake between takeoff and landing, but serious step-by-step lifesaving notes were scribbled on the backside of the photo of the horse I was off to inspect for possible purchase.

Hardly a curl was out of place as we coasted into the western airport, but the hair on the back of my neck stood straight up when I rounded a corner in the terminal and came face-to-face with a five-hundred-pound stuffed grizzly bear. Old Yogi had friends lined up all the way to the luggage pick-up — mountain goats, buffalo, eagles, and, at the end of the line, an over-stuffed bobcat that guarded my suitcase with evil eyes.

Jim was holding a little cardboard sign with my name on it, welcoming me with a polite drawl to his friendly state. Dressed in worn-out jeans and boots the size of my suitcase, he escorted me through the doors while excusing his tardiness as his taxi had needed a wash.

Walking past the short-term and then the long-term parking, I wondered to myself just how big Jim's pickup was that he needed a special carport, when we turned the last corner and I was directed to the open door of a helicopter!

Looking up in a panic, I saw that the safe and secure jet-liner was already flying overhead on its way back east. My stomach turned inside out and tied up tighter than a slipknot around a calf as I stared into the eyes of Big Bird, who was painted on the outside of the flying bubble.

Blanking out most of the 60-mile trip to Jim's ranch, I do remember peeking through one eye long enough to see some awesome country. One feature I determined the west offered that my eastern state didn't was, at birth every child was issued at least two horses. There was a horse in every nook and cranny one could imagine!

Big Bird came to a wingless sliding halt while my stomach had been left somewhere between cloud nine and the airport. No longer excited to see the mare or any other four-legged critter, I froze in place as Jim grabbed a rifle from behind the seat and shot at the ground about 10 feet in front of his taxi. Shocked that I would actually feel "safe" in a helicopter, I heard Jim mumble under his breath something about "rattlesnakes and wolves" while offering me his hand for an exit.

Panicked and estimating the hike to the nearest Amtrak station, I wondered if Jim's western countryside offered a bus service, or maybe a stagecoach…

Got Milk?

It wasn't about the quality of milk that Dan the milkman delivered; it was the quantity. With six kids around the kitchen table, it was pretty crowded without a lot of elbow room, but reaching for food became a lot easier as carton after carton of milk disappeared. Oldest brother became the deal-breaker when he cheated on the rules of "one glass each," doing the pour-and-gulp trick.

Dad's fist landed in the middle of the kitchen table to stunned silence and very wide eyes as he announced that, from then on, our milk would not be delivered in cartons; it would be distributed from a live Holstein cow.

Cows were just great—we had a bunch of them—but the idea of feeding and cleaning up after a special milk-producing appliance didn't go over too well, especially with Mom. When the youngest sister meekly asked how the milkman was going to bring the milk from a cow in the barn to our house, it broke the silence a bit and we all got pretty excited to go "cow shopping."

Seated neatly in the back of the pickup, we six shoppers directed Dad through a pasture full of black and white Holsteins while arguing over which huge milk container looked the finest for our morning cornflakes.

The lead cow moseyed over to check us out and stuck her whole head in the window while letting out a very loud moo. Dad honked the horn to shoo her away, but Ol' Boss, as we immediately named her, stood her ground against the pickup and gave Dad a very gross smooch. Dad was vetoed for any other automatic milk-producing choices, and Boss was delivered to our farm the next day.

Down the line we were elected, oldest first, to be in charge of Boss and deliver the morning milk to Mom. Excited to try out the new giant milk maker, all six of us kids fought over the gleaming silver pail the first morning to be the first to produce our cornflake topping and get on Mom's good side for the day.

We stood around the cow as she happily munched her hay, and fingers pointed all the way around until they stopped at me. Oh, goody cheesecake, I thought to myself as I was the chosen one to "make milk." The girls from "Little House on the Prairie" milked cows, and if Laura Ingalls could do it, so could I. The first lesson that Ol' Boss taught us kids is that you never, ever sit on the stool behind a cow and try for milk. I washed my hair ten times that day, but the stink just wouldn't come out.

Lesson number two ended with little brother plastered against the wall and the pail through the only glass window in the barn. We all knew that horses kicked, but no one had bothered to explain that a horse's "cow kick" originated with Boss. That old gal could kick sideways ten times faster than all of us put together could run forwards.

Dad strolled into the barn just in time to see the world's greatest milking machine ever invented. The dog was assigned "cow alert" at Boss's head; two kids were each wrapped around a back leg, holding it down; the oldest brother was sitting atop the cow for weighted-down kick-proofing; and I was trying my darnedest to make some "real" milk. Dad immediately relieved us of our milking duties and sent us packing to the house so he could "get milk."

Shortly after that, an extra walk-in door to the barn was placed where Dad had gone through the wall. Boss was sent back to her green pasture, and we kids waited happily at the end of the driveway for Dan the milkman's truck to arrive with some good, "old-fashioned" milk...

Traveling with Garmin
Part 1: Continental Divide

Monday, July 13: The plan was to depart on a nice little westward-bound, weeklong vacation by or around 6 a.m.

7:10 a.m.: Our car pulls out of the driveway with Ed and me adjusting seatbacks and seatbelts. The Stanley Thermos is filled to the brim with steaming coffee, while the first of thirty or so chocolate chip cookies is tastefully dunked. Could life get any better?

7:30 a.m.: The car pulls back into the driveway so Ed can collect up his wallet. Funny thing, those forgotten wallets really put a crimp in a happy little send-off.

7:40 a.m.: Ed programs Garmin the GPS Wonder to our faraway destination.

7:45 a.m.: My coffee spills over the center console as I reach over to help Ed with the programming.

7:47 a.m.: We sit a quarter mile from home on the side of the gravel road. Vacation plans are about to be abandoned as Garmin instructs Ed to turn left into a field approach.

9:00 a.m.: The chocolate chip cookie container is empty, but Stanley the Super-Thermos is still pouring steaming hot coffee. Ed needs to pull over for a break, but I require a little more privacy in the midst of passing cars and semis. Forty-five miles to the nearest interstate rest area, Garmin is "recalculating" our time of arrival as Ed spots a heavy-duty tow rope lost along the highway and it's his Christmas in July.

10:00 a.m.: The electric window on the back passenger side blows a gasket and refuses to go up. The Sunday newspaper is flying around the inside of the car in mini-tornado formation and then out the back window, page by page. Garmin states we have to turn right in 1.7 miles, then keep left. Ed and Garmin have quit communicating, and I move the GPS to my side of the car and turn down his volume to protect him from further damage.

11:00 a.m.: Every radio station is scratchy and inaudible. Ed starts singing tunes from "It's a Wonderful Life," and I count the yellow lines (one by one by one).

Noon: In a strange city, Garmin is programmed to find us a hot meal. We are directed to the back door of a butcher shop where the sign reads, "We slay 'em, you eat 'em." I was friends with Garmin up to this point but threatened to replace him with an atlas.

1:00 p.m.: The caution sign reads, "Deer, next 300 miles." Ed pulls out a loaded rifle from under the front seat.

2:00 p.m.: The back passenger window rolls up all by itself and the other three zip down.

2:10 p.m.: As we drive by a crystal-clear lake, a fisherman just happens to be netting a giant trout from shore, and Ed's forehead and hands start sweating. I smile to myself but then plaster my nose to the window as a gorgeous mare and colt trot alongside a fence across the ditch.

3:00 p.m.: The off-ramp signs are starting to read a little strange. Every creek, slough, and gravel road is named after an animal. Garmin has a heart attack at Buffalo Jump Pass.

3:30 p.m.: A few rain clouds to the west sure don't look too threatening, and we laugh at the vehicles pulling over to the sides with clear skies directly above us. Then, in a matter of one mile, the holy mother of rain and hail stops us dead-center on the interstate. Garmin turns blue and dials 911.

4:00 p.m.: Garmin tells us we have a "travel error" as Ed drives over the median, chasing a coyote.

4:15 p.m.: The Dairy Queen had sounded like a refreshing stop, but the sign could have given us a clue we would travel forty-five miles out of our way for a Dilly Bar! Garmin warned us, but we weren't talking to him. As we jumped into a western time zone, the "ice crème drive-up" must have been calculated for the Pacific Ocean for the speedy hour-and-a-half service we received. They must have moseyed out to the pasture, caught the cow, milked her, and made the ice cream—all while we waited very patiently for our delicious, double-chocolate dipped ice cream bars.

5:30p.m.: "Caution: Falling Rocks" signage went ignored, but we should have had a clue when Garmin slid himself under the dash. Ed had piloted expertly around the first loose rocks on the highway, but the wheelbarrow-sized boulder bouncing down the side of the mountain can't be ignored. Sliding to a stop directly in front of us, the mineral-based vacation-stopper breaks into a million non-refundable highway miles. Garmin starts communicating in gibberish while showing a picture on his screen of our car driving sideways in the middle of nowhere with nonexistent roads.

7:00 p.m.: We name the road and spray-paint the rocks "West Cow Rump No-Pass" as we wait for the tow truck to haul us back to an easier time zone...

Traveling with Garmin
Part 2: Divide and Conquer

After recovering from the "You Park It, We'll Repair It" shop, Ed and I made the bold decision to continue west where no Midwestern farm couple has gone before. I had everything in its place, right down to the cute little mule on the dash, moved well out of Ed's reach; it hee-hawed with any right or left motions of the car.

The beverage cooler was packed precisely perpendicular to us on the back floor, a small stainless steel garbage can with pop-up lid was next to it, and all paper paraphernalia was categorized alphabetically in the back center console.

Ed pulled out a bag of pork rinds from the food cooler. One crumb at a time, the little pile on the seat made my blood boil and my pupils dilate.

"Hey Ed, quick, look left at the cool mountain," I said as I scooped up as many crumbs as I could without him noticing. The car dents had been straightened at the garage, but ol' toothless hot-rod mechanic said the windows would have to be fixed at an eastern garage. So, life was just swell as Ed's window zoomed down by itself, seeming to know precisely when each crumb would fall and be blown into the back seat.

We had placed Garmin the GPS Wonder on the back dash as we needed him, but wouldn't let him know it. I swear he displayed a little happy face each time my eyes followed the crumbs blowing his way.

Speeding up on a group of biker-gang look-alike motorcyclists, it makes me nervous as they could just "reach over and nab you," especially if the danged electric window decided to pull one of its shenanigans.

I could tell one of them was a gal from the back, and she was sprawled out on the machine like it was a recliner while cruising 80 down the interstate. The closer we got, the more nervous I was, but Ed seemed to be enjoying his little scenic tour.

Wow and double wow! The gal's gas tank was painted with a herd of running horses in more detail than any da Vinci original. I tried not to stare but couldn't help it. Non-horse person Ed noticed my wee, happy moment in the middle of nowhere and set the cruise down a notch. I think there was a giggle from Garmin on the back dash; he would get his at the next rest stop!

One moment we were a middle-aged married couple minding our own business on a little vacation, and the next—"Ed, ED, EDDDD!" as I grabbed the steering wheel, bringing us out of the ditch as the mule on the dash went into a hee-hawing fit. The biker-gal's poncho had blown over to reveal a set of chaps (chaps don't have rump coverings).

After passing the group, I looked back to make sure we hadn't run over anyone. Garmin was completely swiveled around on his base with smoke coming out of his wires. Two against one—the next 500 miles would be just peachy!

The car had been checked and double-checked with a triple-A rating by Ed, but something was noticeably wrong with the tires and getting worse by the mile. Thank goodness we were coming up on a town without an animal name and pulled into the nearest garage for a wheel balance.

Big O's manager made the toothless wonder mechanic at our last stop seem like Andy Griffith. Oh, we were offered R&R, coffee, and cookies in the waiting area, but I just couldn't bring myself to sit on the wooden bench with an ax sticking out of one end. Ed was having a gas watching five channels at once on the ten-inch television on the end table, and I wondered if he realized it was a small reception problem instead of a high-tech unit.

Out comes Big O from the service area, rubbing his hands together with a crap-eating grin while removing his little calculator from under the counter. Apparently, one of the tires had a small split and Biggie was counting his cash from the out-of-state license plate to bring vittles home to Mama that evening. This would be a showdown similar to the OK Corral as Ed stiffened up when he was told we would need four new tires.

Glancing at the ax, I decided it would be a pretty good idea to move between it and Ed. Driving to the Super Shopco for one new tire while the donut wobbled on the back, Ed was humming music from "The Good, the Bad, and the Ugly." The mule on the dash was howling up a storm from the wobbling car, but Garmin didn't say a word; he knew better...

Traveling with Garmin
Part 3: Divided by Three

I was playing the alphabet game all by myself. Ed and I had been getting along just marvelously the last two hundred miles; I was driving and he was sleeping. Garmin was even tolerable as the interstate was pretty much a straight-ahead, no-turn stretch as far as one wanted to drive. Take away the rolling hills and mountain background, and it would seem just like home.

The letter F had been assigned to a "Freddie's Fresh Fish" truck as I passed, so I gave myself two extra points. G wouldn't give itself up for miles and miles, and no matter how much chatter Garmin spit out from the back dash, I wouldn't count him! Then, there it was—a sign on the side of the interstate pointing north to the City of Garnet. I had forgotten all about me and my sisters' little trip up there about a million years ago. Taking the letter G completely out of my little alphabet game, I started to have hallucinations of the time we three drove an old, beat-up Chevy Nova around and around the curves on the way up, while looking straight down. Going back down on a very muddy Wallace Creek Road after visiting the ghost town that had us spooked to death proved to be the real nightmare.

I sped the car up and kept to the far side of a semi for twenty miles, shaking my head to get the letter G out. Glancing up at the semi driver, I saw he was talking on his CB, probably telling all the other truck drivers to look the heck out for the crazy woman.

Ed woke up almost postmortem, asking where we were and why my face was so white. Tired and crabby, I told him to go back to sleep for another hundred miles or be dropped off at a nice little tourist attraction that started with the letter G. Confused, he rolled his eyes and went back to sleep. Just for the heck of it, I pulled Garmin by the wires to the front seat and programmed the city of Garnet into his cute little window. As he repeated "travel error" over and over, I wondered what he would do if I actually brought him up there.

NASCAR is OK to watch, especially the pit stops when things go wrong like tires and body parts flying all over the place. But when Ed takes it a little too seriously on our vacation fuel stops, the mood gets a little tense. I like to mosey around and look at ridiculously overpriced souvenirs and shiny trinkets, timing my return to the car just right before he blows a head gasket.

Just about to our destination, the altitude got the better of Garmin and he spouted off directions, sounding like Alvin the chipmunk. The car also had a little trouble with the altitude and lost ground to a Volkswagen on the upside of a pass. Ed stated for the hundredth time, "We should have taken the pickup," while I sat back and enjoyed my souvenir bag of rock candy and whisky creek malto drink.

Happy, happy and hugs, hugs as we were greeted at the door by relatives, and then we all sat down and stared at one another. "How was your trip?" wasn't a great start for conversation and we all ate supper in silence.

A fresh morning brought an invitation from an elderly neighbor gal for a boat ride; both Ed and I agreed it might be a nice day for it. We just looked at each other as the waves splashed in from the other side of the lake twenty-five miles across; Ed made sure his life jacket was buckled up, and I put on three.

Thinking the itsy bitsy little old lady would just putt-putt around the lakeshore, we climbed aboard for a leisurely tour. Holy moly and great tides a-turning!—Captain Speedy jammed the throttle full bore! I tried to climb into the bait container but wouldn't fit, and Ed just sat back and watched the shore go further and further away.

Rounding the turn into a bay, both Ed and I waited for our stomachs to catch up as our captain asked if we would like to see actor John Lithgow's cabin. Trying not to show my excitement, the little "yep" came out sheepishly as our western tour guide stood up in the boat and yelled, "Hey, John, ya home?" Looking at the bait compartment again, I knew there was nowhere to hide if Big John actually came out to greet us, but Speedy was insistent and pulled right up to his dock! Dang if our little grey-haired guide didn't pounce out and go waddling down the shore to find us an actor to meet.

Taking advantage of our paparazzi moment, the camera was immediately hauled out and turned to fast-flash mode to capture each and every inch of Big John's landing: two jet-skis, an impressive pontoon with a yellow lattice around the top, and a dock the size of kingdom come. Looking through the lens, I was so impressed with what my photo shoot caught next: horses—three of them! Speedy came trotting down the dock, saying no one was home but she had placed a note on the door with our names and phone number so John could call and say "hey" to his missed visitors. This time I did crawl into the bait container.

Our time out west went way too fast as most vacations do. The morning of departure was hectic as Ed wanted to get an early start. I didn't think it was necessary for him to get up at five a.m. and rotate the tires, but who was I to say anything. Aunt Kate let him have it, though.

As Ed tossed the suitcases into the trunk in a messy way, I made an excuse in order to go re-arrange them—you know, my little neat fetish. As I hid behind the trunk lid, Garmin scowled at me through the window as the lady kept telling me to speak up. Ducking and whispering a little louder into my cell phone, I asked her to please tell me again the price of an eastward-bound plane ticket...

Trailer Backing – 101

Moving livestock from point A to point B requires persons on horseback and a few thousand acres of open range (or a pickup and trailer). The latter has been our only option for years as the local law enforcement gets pretty excited when they see cattle being herded down the highway.

To this day I just can't use the mirrors to back the most wonderful animal limousine, though I've given it a dang good try a few times. Like the day I was backing an eight-foot-wide trailer into a ten-foot-wide barn. As I watched the trailer in the side mirrors, it was slow and steady going; I amazed even myself as first the trailer and then the pickup backed in straight as an arrow. Then, as I was looking in the rear view mirror with a foot or so to go, taking note of my bad hair day and straightening my collar, crash! We must remember to leave room for the outside mirrors. Good thing it was close to dark as Uncle Curt borrowed our pickup the next day and all blame was placed on his side of the fence.

I've always said, give a horse forty acres of pasture with one small piece of old machinery in the far corner and the horse will find it and cut himself. Give Emily a forty-acre farm with one water hydrant out in the open and she will back a trailer over it. Old Faithful felt great on that hot and humid August day (until the well ran dry).

One of my very first hauling experiences was taking a load of critters to an auction market way out of my comfort zone. This was Ed's job, but he had made the feeble excuse that combining grain that day was essential as rain was expected. It did rain, but only on my little parade at the end of the day.

Getting to the far-away auction was the easy part; finding the right chute and backing the trailer to it was a nightmare, to say the least.

There must have been a hundred or so livestock trailers in various stages of loading and unloading, and drivers leaning alongside their pickups chatting and spitting snoose, all happy and having a great day. When I saw the line I was to be in and where I had to back the trailer, I just about turned around and high-tailed it home. A building on one side with a fence on the other and a narrow sixty-foot distance to the chute — Calgon, take me away!

I looked around for female counterparts; there had to be at least one other gal waiting to back into the chute to screw it up before I did. Nope, all guys, and all were watching Emily as it was my turn to unload. This was by far one of the worst moments in my entire life!

Thank goodness there was a pair of gloves on the seat as my hands were sweating so bad they were slipping off the steering wheel. As my mirror viewing was a little problem, I casually put my right arm up along the top of the seat, looking back over my shoulder and pretending I knew perfectly well what I was doing.

Remember Thumper's foot in the movie "Bambi"? That's what my right foot was doing on the gas pedal and I couldn't stop it! Driving a clutch, there was no option of using the (still slightly calm) left foot, and all I could think was that this out-of-control extremity would thump one last time and stay down on the gas. We sure as heck wouldn't have to worry about the loading chute then, as it would be part of my trailer.

"Our Father who art in Heaven" is the last thing I remember; the rest of the unloading process has been blanked out of my mind "forever and ever." All I know is that when I came home with an empty trailer, Ed asked how the trip went, and for some strange reason my right leg started twitching...

Close the Door

Our house cats are probably like everyone else's... or maybe not. I've explained how orphan Lucy, "the Boy Named Sue," came to be one of our family members. Smoke came to us as a troublesome teen who needed a home, but how does a person begin to explain what goes on behind closed doors?

"Nice kitty, kitty, I promise not to move while you're lounging on my lap for fear of a ten-claw retaliation."

"Please, Smoke, don't jump from the couch to my shoulder again when I'm not looking and then try to hang on as I'm being ripped apart."

The long meow followed by two short mini-meows in the middle of the night means Lucy would like to go outside, and no amount of tossing or turning shuts him up until he's out the door. Awhile later, he's hanging by his claws on the bedroom screen window, howling for all he's worth to be let back inside.

Smoke's a little more tolerant of my sleep until Lucy's in and settled down; then fifteen pounds of cat jump from the dresser onto my head, letting me know it's his turn for the door. Smoke is very fond of leaping and was pretty amusing at it when he was younger, but now he resembles a wannabe flying elephant.

Ever tie a string to a blade of the ceiling fan and watch your pretty cats play merry-go-round? Ever see a cat go at this so hard he pants and then pukes?

The old fish tank phenomenon is cute as a bug's ear as the handsome young feline bats at the tank glass, playing tag with the fish. It's not so funny when said cat actually dives inside the tank, sloshes around until he's made his choice of goldfish, and then "buries" it under the bed.

Get the tilted-head look, open the door, and patiently wait until the cat decides if the weatherman was just kidding, or if it's still winter. Get the look again an hour later and repeat steps one and two. Nope, it's still winter. The third daily trip to the door in winter is always a charm as the snow is once again daintily tested with a paw, the claws extend to go along with mean dilated eyes, and you are sideswiped as the sweet little pet trots back and jumps onto the recliner you were sitting in.

One of those inventions that should have been isolated to a warm, dry climate claiming no creepy crawlers or rodents is the easy-entry, easy-exit "pet door."

Most decisions and purchases here are well thought-out in advance with all angles and "for instances" taken into consideration. On the plus side of installing our pets' personal in/out access, anytime during the day or night, the little kitty door would provide uninterrupted sleep for us and would eliminate the multiple daily trips to and from the front door.

If cats are supposed to be so smart, why did it take two full months of traipsing to the door day and night to gently push open the supposed-to-be-easy-entry/exit cat-sized panel for them? If you build it, they will come — sure, but could they figure out how to use it instead of giving you the look?

After the initial training-in period, life was good as both cats strolled in and out at will, keeping their "looks" to a minimum in front of the food dish when it was empty. Then it rained. The muddy paw tracks from the cat door to the food dish and then to the couch would not be tolerated, and their personal-entry access was barred until further sunshine. Again, how smart is a cat that continues to attempt suicide by plowing head-first into a pint-sized locked door?

With the rainy season over and the yard dried up, the little cat door was unbarred, letting loose two very happy felines.

Ever sing this silly song as a youngster — "Great big gobs of greasy grimy gopher guts, marinated monkey feet, French-fried parakeet..."? Well, we didn't get the monkey, but we did get the gopher and parakeet parts. How does one explain to pampered little kitties that rodent remains should be fully consumed before entering the house? I'm not afraid of mice, but when a fifteen-pound cat is playing soccer with a live, squeaking one on top of my covers at midnight, those little bitty eyes look pretty dang terrifying.

When I was ready to bar the not-so-well-thought-out pet door, Ed talked me into giving the cats one last chance.

Looking out the kitchen window, I didn't have time to block the pet door as Lucy came running, hell-bent for election, up the front steps and through his little door with a rabbit in his mouth almost bigger than he was. As he blocked me from retrieving his catch, the very unhappy cotton-tail was released beside the stove while the cat and I had a long stare-down. No, no way was I going to cook Lucy up a pot of rabbit stew! I was shunned by the cats for two weeks after rescuing Lucy's "happy meal" and nailing their little swinging door shut for good.

The next bright idea that is brought up in this home will be triple-tested against "for instances"…

Communication Gap

We really do try hard to please our fellow citizens, but sometimes it just plain stinks to be polite.

A few years ago, a local agency called to ask if they could bring out a family of recent immigrants to visit the farm. Sure, why not, and God Bless America. We had a pleasant couple of hours showing the family around, letting the kids sit on a horse, pet a calf, and help feed the pigs. When the interpreter thanked us for the tour, the Papa smiled, shook Ed's hand, and said one word — "pieces" — with a huge grin on his face as he got in the car. I looked at Ed and shrugged my shoulders, thinking "pieces" must have meant "thanks" in their language. But, as we found out later, "pieces" was an alternative word for "pork."

"HONK, HONK, HONK" is what we woke up to the next Sunday morning just after daybreak. Somehow, the immigrants had found their way back to our farm by themselves and were sitting in the car, blaring the horn.

Ed was not a very happy camper as we were smack dab in the middle of harvest and he hadn't gone to sleep more than four hours before. I, on the other hand, poured a cup of coffee and courteously walked out to see what our visitors wanted at five in the morning. Now, sometimes I have a hard time deciphering the cooking directions on a box of Rice-a-Roni or programming a remote control, but trying to understand the immigrants' wishes was way over my head.

After a very long game of charades, my coffee was getting cold and both Papa settler and I were having a spaz attack of frustration. For the life of me, I couldn't figure out why Papa was thanking me over and over again while eating an imaginary chicken leg.

Finally, a young boy emerged from the car and spoke ever so slowly the words, "Pieces ... mean ... pork." OK, so we had a bunch of dang pigs on the farm, it was nice to see you again, and please drive safely on the way back to town.

As I headed back to the house, it dawned on me like a ton of bricks what the new settlers were after: a pig!

Sending Ed out the door to deal on a prime porcine for our new friends brought to my mind just too good a picture not to tag along and see how he would manage the task. Apparently, speaking English was not on the top of the list for our local agency, but teaching the value of a dollar had sunk in very well. Watching Ed and Papa chat back and forth in a language only the two of them could understand, I stood in utter amazement.

The immigrants had Ed over a barrel in a matter of minutes with a sale price, and off they trotted to the barn to collect up a "piece."

Curiosity kills the cat, but there was no way I was going to miss the end of this amusing morning. Following within hearing distance, I listened to Ed tell Papa a joke. Laughing hysterically, Papa returned a joke to Ed and the two of them giggled all the way into the barn.

Thinking back to grammar school, by this time I was really second-guessing myself on the language Mrs. Lillibridge forgot to teach our class. That must have been the semester I was locked up in the coat closet for bringing my horse into the third-grade classroom for show-and-tell—he pooped beside her desk.

Papa immigrant selected a prize porcine specimen for their barbeque and placed him in the back part of the mini-van for the ride back to town. I just shook my head and reminded myself of the "don't ask, don't tell" rule while the settlers drove off.

Still a little confused and befuddled at Ed's amazing hidden language talent, I was trying very hard not to look him in the eye when he started laughing with tears pouring down. It's catchy when another person is in such good spirits, and I laughed along with him, not knowing why.

Pointing to the plowed field, Ed sat right down on the ground while wiping the tears away. The subject of his laughter was driving bumpi-ty, bumpity at a fast pace through the field on their way back to the city. The immigrants' country of origin must not have had very good road markers or perhaps no roads at all. After a quarter mile or so, the mini-van made a large loop and the settlers headed back our way. It was about impossible to compose ourselves by this time, but as Papa drove through the yard and onto the road, doing fishtails, he was also laughing and yelled through the open window, "Love de America, be back for more pieces!" in a language we both understood all too well spelled the end of future Sunday morning rest...

Textbook of Tricks

Teaching animals tricks isn't too difficult; the first thing I learned was to never go by the book.

I purchased an incredible two-hundred pager once: "Train Your Horse in Five Easy Lessons" — to say yes and count. According to the manuscript, the horse was supposed to nod its head up and down to say "yes" and paw the ground for each instructed number. I followed all the directions carefully, but after thirty lessons, my pony ended up shaking his head "no" and lying down instead. That was all right, though; I played dumb and showed everyone my amazing trickster every chance I got.

A lady came out to the farm one time to pick up a couple of advertised free barn cats and asked if they were trained mousers. I didn't dare say there wouldn't be much left of them if they couldn't catch a mouse as that was the main staple in their diet. I really needed to cut down on the cat herd, so I offered what she wanted to hear, and she drove out of the yard happy as a lark with the story that I hauled the cats out to the trees each morning for a private hunting lesson. The gal also believed that any mouse seen scooting around on her property would be promptly caught by any of the cats with the words, "Sic 'im!"

We had a couple of big old fat blue jays stealing the dog's food from his dish on the front porch. It was usually in the mornings when they would sit in the tree waiting for the dog to leave and then would fly down, grab a piece of dog chow, and take off again with their sunrise meal.

Little Miss Trick-Trainer here devised a plan to show the kids some amazingly clever feathered fowl. Leaving the dog bowl empty, I would wait till the blue jays came in for chow; there I was, ready with my hand out the door a ways, tossing a morsel to them. After a few practice rounds, the kids were called to the kitchen window and instructed to watch the "Bird Whisperer" in action. In an instructional voice, I summoned any hungry blue jays in the county to fly on in for breakfast. Right on cue, first one and then the other kibbles-and-bits thief swooped out of the tree for their handouts. The kids didn't give me one lick of trouble that whole summer, thinking their mother could call in a bird at any moment to peck their hair out if their chores weren't done.

We raise our own boars, and as they mature, they tend to go wherever they want or through any sorting board in front of them once they're let out of the fence. Ed asked me one day if it was possible to train the young ones to come to a whistle so they would be easier to move around to different pens when they got older. I purchased a bag of animal crackers, and put the "Charlotte's Web" theory into place immediately. Working with the young ones twice a day, I devised a low-to-high-pitch whistle followed by an animal-cracker offering. It didn't take more than a couple of days before I had all the little Wilburs running for their treat and squealing with delight. Ed was impressed, I was impressed, and all was well with the world.

As the little ones grew into fine young gentlemen, I would whistle and give them a treat every month or so to keep up the training. When they got old enough to move into the rest of the herd, a little whistle had them trotting right along behind me across the yard towards the correct pen.

Well, guess what? Wilbur and his two brothers all came down with huge "attention deficit disorder" when they got close to the "girls'" side of the fence. As they went scattering all over the place, my little march to the pen fell into a terrible disorder! Somehow, Ed got in the middle of the catastrophe and yelled for all he was worth for me to "Whistle 'em down!" as Wilbur #1 looked at him with some real serious "girlie eyes."

From my safe view atop a fence post, it looked like Ed was toast as I tried to make the correct whistle, but all that came out was a high-pitched honking noise because I was laughing too dang hard to get serious. About that time, Uncle Curt came strolling out of the shop, happy as could be, as his new combine header was in and he was off to collect it up. When Uncle Curt is happy, he whistles…

Prairiewood Condominiums

I just about hit the ditch the other day when driving by the neighbors' place to the north. In the front yard, they're building a playhouse for the kids that looks to be about the size of a double garage! It's got all the bells and whistles — attached playground, mini-golf, and a water slide. Heck, all they needed was five-hundred bales of hay and their kids would have had the playhouse of their dreams!

Us girls couldn't wait until the first hay was stacked; it was prime untouched real estate. We'd start removing and rearranging the top bales from the back side so Dad couldn't see us, and by the time our condos were finished, all he could do was shake his head and swear at the dog.

Stairs were a single bale at a time; little sister had to have the bottom apartment as she only dared climb three bales high. Hallways were well-lit with the world's greatest skylight, and doors were always unlocked but "never ever" could we enter another's home-sweet-home without the imaginary knock. Tea parties and ballroom dances were held daily by us homesteading tenants, each taking turns entertaining.

Refrigerators were the original stainless steel upright hay bale version, fully stocked with whatever one's imagination could dream up. One bale was a single bed, two a full, and if there was enough room in your condo's bedroom, a three-bale, king-sized bed with double headboards was included.

A big rock turned into a beautiful bronze statue on a single-bale dining room table, and dandelions made perfect yellow-rose centerpieces.

When Dad needed to remove some of our building with the tractor and loader to feed the cattle, he was thoughtful enough to remove the "undeveloped" section of our condominiums first.

One year we had an especially well-organized town/field home and figured out a brainstorm of an idea to keep it into the winter rather than the cows getting it. We cut the twine, taking half the hay out, and, with the leftover tying material, made two bales out of one. Dad would come for his ten bales a day to feed the cows and we could keep our lovely apartments!

Not thinking more than five minutes ahead on any given day, we proceeded to cut all the top bales open to double the stack. When that was finished, we cut into the second layer to mix the hay in with the first. Getting some dang nice, tight, fifteen-pound bales, we ran out of twine. The third layer of hay was then chopped up along with a disappearing building and three young "Einsteins."

Mom's clothesline was used for the fourth layer, and the top wire of the cattle fence was cut up for the fifth. Our building was trashed, we couldn't call FEMA, and we were in BIG trouble!

Sister "Know-it-all" suggested we take another row of cow fence, along with some steel posts, and make a corral around the haystack. We would then chase all the cows into it and show Dad our brilliant new idea of "self-feeding," and he would then praise us through Sunday for the time-saving feeding technique!

What we didn't think of was the "grass is always greener" theory. There was NO way those cows were going anywhere but the alfalfa field across the road. Our simple tea party that morning turned into a demolished haystack with cattle roaming the countryside and no fence to put them back into.

Maybe my neighbors to the north didn't have such a bad idea after all...

Seasonal Disorganization

They call it deer-hunting season, but I call it the time of year when Ed and a bunch of other guys get zombie-eyed and bungle-brained.

It would make no sense at all to plan ahead and ready one's hunting equipment a week or two in advance. Oh no, everything must be done the night before in a mad dash, and look the heck out if anyone gets in the way or suggests a different approach to the order of preparation.

Hard-boiled eggs, the main staple of deer hunting, are a necessity and must be a guy thing, like turkey is to Thanksgiving. Twelve hard-boiled eggs for each hunter, and that's just for one day. Reminded one year by Ed that the "other guy's wife" peeled and diced her husband's eggs, I packed his twelve little treats nice and neat in the cooler — unboiled.

Like clockwork each year, it's the mad dash to town, walking in for licenses at the last possible moment before the store closes. Then it's the stop at the grocery store for the munchy part of the weekend's diet. Pickled herring, candy bars, pork rinds, multi-packages of cookies, and let's not forget the smoked turkey legs.

I tried to pack a decent meal once: huge ham sandwiches with lettuce and mayonnaise followed by cute little pudding cups for dessert. But when I saw the dog trotting by with a corner of the plastic baggie in his mouth before the guys even took off, I suspended that offering for good.

Of course, all the orange clothing from the year before is either lost, mangled beyond repair, or conveniently outdated, and a trip to the sporting goods store is required. One year when I met up with the crew on the road during an egg break, the biggest, toughest hunter of the party walked around the side of the pickup carrying a shotgun with a price tag dangling from his carrot-colored hat. Calling him Phyllis Diller, I ran like all get-out to my car before I could be shot at.

The pickups are shined up from one end to the other, and belongings that have been lost for a year are surprisingly found. One young neighbor proposed to his future bride at daybreak before rushing off to hunt because he found the engagement ring he had purchased the year before under the pickup seat.

That commitment is still on hold.

After the pickup is spic-and-span, the guns are taken out for spiffing up and residue removal. The same story is told each year at this cleaning time, of how Grandpa used the old shotgun to track for days on end the largest deer ever mounted in the county. Grandma tells the story a bit differently, with the ending being a pricy new front pickup bumper and a ticket for speeding.

Dad used to travel "way up north" to hunt deer and would come home some years with his booty already wrapped in packages. Mom knew he stopped at the local market that sold deer chops on his way home, but she always complimented him on the freshness and superior taste of the northern deer.

It's a "my truck's bigger than your truck" thing when the dilemma of collecting a deer from the middle of a muddy field occurs. Some of these guys would put the monster-truck show to shame, as they're drop-dead serious about which one can reach the deer first. Who cares about a measly little transmission, much less shocks or broken body parts?

Ed didn't realize a few years ago that the game warden was driving the same exact make and model as his pickup. The poor guy stopped home about noon to say no one would hunt with him. Apparently, each time he spotted his buddies and started driving toward them, they all took off like cats with their tails on fire.

It's a pecking order when it comes to walking or spotting. The younger you are, the more you walk to flush out the deer for the spotters. Ed used to come home complaining, covered in mud with cockleburs stuck to every inch of his clothing. Now, he comes home complaining of his aches and pains from standing beside a stupid tree all day.

Oh, don't we just love the season…

Soup or Salad?

It happened again. With twenty bales of hay left in the barn, I reminded myself to start looking for more. An endless, thankless job I would welcome anyone else to take care of for me. Down to two bales, I procrastinated, hoping the "hay genie" would magically appear with a couple hundred squares to tide my horses over nicely.

How many do you have for sale, is it covered, green, first, second or third cutting, and how much do the bales weigh? Oh, and is it this year's hay or last? Seems like I've asked those questions a hundred times to various hay growers, knowing that maybe one in twenty or thirty might be on the up and honest side with their descriptions over the phone.

Driving an hour or two to "take a peek and smell" of my horses' lunch before buying it was mandatory after I'd had a few bad batches delivered. And of course if it wasn't a hundred and ten degrees, it just wouldn't be worth it now, would it?

I had a "steady eddy" supplier a few years ago. Mr. Jones had baled hay for years and knew how to put up the best. Jones would call a week or two before baling and let me know the approximate date. I could then line up loading and hauling help, have enough hay for the whole year and be a very happy camper. When Mr. Jones started baling his beautiful hay in big round bales, he downright wrecked our tidy relationship. Begging and pleading for small squares was out of the question; he had defected to the other side!

"Second cutting, alfalfa/grass mix in fifty-pound bales," the gentleman relayed ever so nicely. Sounded pretty good to me. "Okey-dokey, I'll be there in about an hour to take a look." Dusty, coarse, and two leaves of alfalfa to a bale just didn't work. Not wanting to tell the fellow his hay "stunk," I told him I had one other batch to check out and would get back to him. Never ever give out your name and phone number to a potential hay seller unless you purchase. Word travels fast and you're recorded on the blacklist of fussy horse-loving broads.

"Perfect June grass put up tight in fifty- to sixty-pound bales." Ohhhh, I could smell it through the phone! I'll be right there! Dang if the guy wasn't right; it was very nice, fresh, green hay today, but by the end of the week after it dried out, I would be able to lift the twines up to my neck and what was left of the bale would maybe weigh twenty pounds. "I'll get back to you."

"Brome grass, pleasantly mixed with one-third alfalfa: horse candy at its best!" Yahoo, this was it! "Sir, I'll be there in thirty minutes. Please don't consign it to anyone until I arrive." Looked good, smelled good, decent weight, and he had plenty. "May I open one up to take a little peek?" "Well, Miss, this here hay is two dollars a bale and if I open one up I'll never get the twines back on tight and won't be able to sell it." That's about the time I spotted the snake head sticking out of a corner of the bale. "I'll get back to you." Where there's one snake, there's a whole lot more!

Second cutting, straight alfalfa, heavy squares. "Just set aside ten and I'll pick them up later this evening and leave a check if you're not around." I knew this neighbor, and as much as I didn't like feeding straight alfalfa, it would do for now until I could find some grass or a mix. Problem—BIG problem: I couldn't lift the dang bales into the pickup! One fellow's version of "heavy" and the next guy's was unbelievable; these bales must have weighed a hundred pounds or more.

The only help I found on the farm was the guy's dog, and the only ambition he seemed to have was burying my check in a hole around the corner of the barn.

Amazing idea—just totally amazing: cutting the bales open and stacking the hay in layers in the back of the pickup.

I should have known better when the bales "popped" as I cut the twines. Flake after flake, I wound up with a total of three whole bales stacked in a pyramid.

As I drove down the highway on the way home, a semi's side wind blew out all but the bottom five flakes.

Just another day, Emily, just another day…

Hey, Mom

Dreaming of the upcoming Mother's Day, I figured I would have a glorious holiday from sun-up to sundown. Triple-chocolate cake would be served on a silver platter at daybreak, and a dozen roses in a vase would replace the alarm clock on the side table.

A 52-inch television would be placed at the end of the bed with a single remote control that selected a hundred channels, every one of them Lifetime.

I would listen to the sounds in the rest of the house: both the dishwasher and the vacuum cleaner running smoothly, the washing machine on a very quiet and non-threatening spin cycle.

Ahhh, someone had already placed a pot roast in the oven for later, and I could also smell a hint of strawberry shortcake in the making.

A rustle outside the window brought my attention to the sparkling clean white horse that had already been saddled and was patiently awaiting a quiet afternoon ride down the lane. Dang, even the saddle bags were packed with carrots for the horse on one side and an assortment of mini-candy bars for me on the other.

"WAKE UP, EMILY, the cows are out!"

Who was it that made that ridiculous quote, something about dreams and having a life? Great expectations, maybe that was it.

Okey-dokey, cows, since you have all ruined my day, perhaps someone would take the cow theme for Mother's Day and grill up a few burgers while Mom puts her feet up. Pancakes and sausage were Ed's choice for brunch; no problem, one of my top ten favorites.

No, no, no, no, don't put the batter in the blender! You stir it softly like this and then let it rest for a bit while the griddle gets hot. No, no, no, don't fry the sausage on high! Simmer it on low like this and turn it often so it browns evenly. No, no, no, don't fry the eggs in oil! Add a dash of butter first like this.

As I served up the family brunch, there was something totally wrong with this picture… a completely unfocused photograph!

I didn't expect many gifts or extra-special days from most of my adopted charges. The two miniature donkeys were a real testimonial to the term "mother," though: Those little buggers continually got into more trouble than they were worth, especially the night before a very important horse show when they decided an explicitly groomed show horse needed some midnight exercise and showed him how to unlatch his stall gate. If that wasn't bad enough, they taught the show horse how to make mud pies while lying down and rolling!

Ed about had a heart attack the day Mother Emily came walking down the driveway with six little black-and-white Peppy La Pews following close behind. Sharing the parenting responsibility with the black-and-white mother cat, we had a nice, tidy little family for quite a while, until the dog barked. Even the pigs received a tomato juice bath that day to get rid of the smell.

Lucy, my orphaned male cat (long story in another column) makes every day Mother's Day. I really try to thank him for the field mice and gopher gifts he brings home, but sometimes we mothers just have to draw the line.

Ed still swears up and down that one year he bought me roses and a mushy card for Mother's Day but left them on the front porch after the emergency phone call. I just don't think that a tractor on fire is more important than bringing your lovely wife gifts, and to this day I won't let out that the goat was mysteriously too full to eat her evening grain.

There's a teenage son in our house that would get mad if I used his real name, so instead of Dustin, I'll call him Dan.

A couple of years ago, Dan signed up for something in school and replaced his real name (Dan) with his social nickname, "Big Dog."

A few weeks later we received a letter from a prestigious university informing Big Dog that he was more than welcome to attend classes at their fine school.

"To Mr. and Mrs. Big Dog: Your son has been chosen to attend Florida State" was another nice how-do-you-do.

Check this out: "Dear Mr. Big Dog, We have located your extended relatives in Ireland and, for a small fee, will send you a complete name and photo family tree of the Dog family." Ed didn't think it was too funny, but I, on the other hand, just about sent for the "Dog Family Tree" just to see what our Irish relations looked like…

Three's a Crowd

Our ride was an old beaten-up Chevy Nova, and our destination was northwest Montana to a cousin's wedding.

My two sisters and I had planned our mini-vacation for months, precisely calculating each hour and mile to get the most out of our wonderful vacation getaway.

Jill, the oldest, would drive the first few hundred miles as Barb, the youngest, read the map, and I would sleep until my turn to navigate the way west as we planned to carry on straight through. Neither Jill nor I trusted Barb's driving after the hit-and-run incident with a county sheriff's vehicle.

Somewhere in the middle of North Dakota, Barb became dreadfully quiet and turned a pale shade of greenish grey. Of course, Jill and I thought it was hilarious that Barb was getting car sick until it became a reality right down the middle of I-94. While I was trying to navigate the Nova, hanging halfway out the window for air, Jill was holding the passenger door open and gagging up a storm. Luckily, a rest stop was near and Barb was banned from the car until she could hold her lunch in. This delay was not on our agenda, and the beauty of the Medora wilderness was beheld well after dark. Barb acquired the nickname of "Upchuck" — which positioned a permanent scowl on her face.

At the tourist viewing area overlooking the great caverns and colors of the wilderness, we all took pictures anyway. Who cared if it was pitch dark?

Tired and travel-weary, we all three decided to indulge in just a "short" nap on the benches at the edge of the overlook since onlookers were sparse in the viewing area. About an hour later, Jill must have had one of her "spider" dreams as she lit up off the bench in a screaming fit and slid right through the fence rails over and down, and down, and down. Barb started crying that she would never see her big sister again, and, angry that our trip was yet again postponed, I explained to a hysterical Barb, "Yes, Jill will be back; there is food in the car." We could smell her before she topped the ridge, and for the rest of our journey, Jill's nickname would be "Buffalo Poop."

While reading the map as Barb slept in the back seat and Jill had a sunflower seed spitting contest with herself while driving, I spotted a tiny star right off the Interstate with the golden words "Ghost Town" next to it. I explained to my sisters that their two delays had cost us valuable traveling time already, and this little sightseeing adventure would only cost us a half-hour at the most.

Understanding, but rolling their eyes, they granted my wish to see a Ghost in a Town at the top of a mountain. The map read that Garnet, Montana, was just a mile or two away, and after a few vertical S-turns, the clay road turned into a hiking trail with a straight-down drop-off. With no room to turn around, we ventured on and up as my sisters were now agreeing that to see the abandoned gold-mining town and maybe the ghost of "Wild Bill" Hickock would be a great highlight of our vacation.

Passing a corral of cows, the three of us agreed that the owner must feed them by helicopter as there was no way those cows could navigate the steep terrain, much less find any grass. Some time later, we decided they were "ghost cows."

After well over an hour of forging up the mountain, Jill sarcastically invented the name "Pilot Parker," referring to my guiding skills. Blaming a misprint on the map for my guiding dilemma, I agreed to attempt turning around as it had started raining and the ghosts would probably want to stay inside and warm since the temperature was also falling.

After a twenty-five-point turnaround, each one of us started blaming the other for our dreadful vacationing low-lights until the Nova started slip-sliding atop the wet clay on the way down the mountain. Screaming and crying at the same time, Barb ended up white-knuckled behind the wheel while Jill and I walked to avoid certain death over the drop-off. Jill's flip-flops turned into "flip-offs," and I sported thirty pounds of clay packed onto each one of my boots. Barb would never be the same after a huge evergreen stopped both her and the Nova from sliding over the mountainside on the last S-turn.

Exhausted, covered in mud, and not speaking to one another, Buffalo Poop, Upchuck, and Pilot Parker walked into the wedding chapel as the last bell tolled.

In a recent "remember when" conversation, the three of us laughed and reminisced about our long-ago journey. I kept silent my fears of touching a map or getting near a red gemstone; Jill and I didn't comment on Barb's permanent white knuckles; and eldest sister would never, ever tell anyone that she tied herself to the bed at night for fear of falling while she slept…

Sidetracked

About three hours ago, I sat down here with a chocolate milkshake and a purring cat on my lap in full "Outhouse" mode with an amusing tale to tell. Starting out with "Once upon a time," you were going to hear of the one and only occasion Emily rode a Holstein bull in the County Fair "Western-pleasure" class, but one blasted telephone call put everything on hold.

No, Ed, you did not put the receipt for your bottle of (I can't even pronounce the name of it) hog medication on my desk earlier today. Yes, dear, I looked in your coat pockets, on the kitchen counter beside the half-full milk carton you left out at lunch, and even on the floor in the bathroom beside the toilet.

No, dear, the receipt was not outside on the porch beside the muddy boots that had first tracked half-ways into the kitchen before backing up in the same footprints to try to cover yourself.

Yes, dear, I will check my desk again. Did you put it in your wallet?

Dropping the phone and reaching down to retrieve it, I noticed that there, under the corner of my desk, was the long-lost earring I had given up for dead.

Happy as a lark to unite the two earrings in my jewelry box, I saw, tucked between the ring holders empty of diamond rings, the folded-up receipt for my very first horse trailer. Reminiscing about the day I pulled that shiny black trailer home and tried to hide it behind the barn, I got the silly notion to compare features to our latest trailer purchase and see how times had changed.

Back at my desk, rummaging through the file drawers, I found the newest trailer receipt but tossed it aside when I came across a packet of old "Important Receipts" with "Do Not Throw" written with big red marker.

I wondered about the scribbled president's signature on the Hampshire certificate that supposedly indicated a century-long guarantee for the black-and-white piglets I have not seen in our barn for a very, very long time, even though it's only been a mere twenty years.

Oh, look — registration papers for a coon dog that was scared to death of the dark. Ed trudged half-ways across the country to collect up the pedigreed mutt named Sir Geronimo to fulfill his childhood dream. I think he read "Where the Red Fern Grows" one too many times as a youngster and truly believed there was a coon up every tree and an expensive hound from a faraway land would actually come out of his kennel at night to hunt with him. Geronimo was one heck of a rural-mail-carrier chaser, but we won't tattle about that or dwell on the letters thrown out the car window at forty miles per hour.

Out of the packet slipped a business card from a feed dealer I hadn't thought about in years. That old fart would come around every month, wheeling and dealing his newest formula for fat and sassy cows, along with a secret recipe for the slickest market hogs ever produced. He freely furnished samples of his "Sure Grow," along with "before" and "after" photos of his happy clients' fruitful livestock, until Ed finally gave in and ordered a pallet of the animal-enhancing formula. Measuring and feeding the required amounts to all the farm's livestock for a month, neither Ed nor I saw one bit of difference. Mad as a wet hen, Ed gave me the go-ahead to sic the dog on the crook the next time he came around. In town for supplies not long after that, following the lad carrying my groceries to the car, I spotted Mr. Feed Dealer by his truck, scooping oatmeal from a super-sized bag into little bags labeled "Sure Grow." When our eyes met, I thought the poor fellow's jaw was going to hit the ground and he would need a not-yet-invented Depends undergarment. Needless to say, "Sure Grow" was not grown in our part of the woods from then on.

A picture and pedigree of "Hickory Smoke on Hoofs" stuck out from the back of the packet, bringing my daydreaming to an end as that old Holstein bull was supposed to be the main story line here.

Ed called and said he had found the receipt in his wallet…

How'd That Happen?

It was a nice day for travel, and as much as I hate driving to town, even the traffic didn't bother me. The old grey gelding was out of his special feed mix, and even at thirty degrees below with six feet of snow, I would have made the trip for my good old friend.

Pulling up to the shop at home, I saw the usual after-five crowd milling about telling the same stories and blending up the same chronicles they had the week before. Every once in a while there's a new happening and the story is hours old by "shop time" with many, many versions for days and years to come.

Ed must have just finished his tale of the time the immigrants came out to our farm to purchase a hog as he was laughing so hard he was crying while explaining how the poor newcomer wanted water and his hand-pumping charades resembled something else.

Nick had his chest pushed up and out, and I could see he was about to tell the tale of how he caught the gigantic northern with his bare hands; that always comes directly after the half-hour story of his boat capsizing in the middle of a thunderstorm.

Ray was kicking gravel around with his left foot, meaning the economic revolution of diesel engines was on the tip of his tongue, ready to be explained to all whether they wanted to hear it again or not.

I nodded nicely, pretending to be semi-interested in all conversation and fables, but my glances toward the bags of horse feed and my silent wishes for a helpful hand were dismissed with "the flood of '67."

As I hefted a bag of feed out of the trunk, Nick came from around the third-tree-to-the-right restroom and said in passing that a four-wheeler would come in real handy to haul my feed to the barn.

There was immediate silence, head-scratching, and chaw-spitting while Nick's words sank into the group, and then everyone started talking at the same time, giving advice about four-wheelers. Old, new, used, and abused — all makes and models were contemplated and disputed.

The next morning as we were having coffee at the kitchen table, Ed told his cup that one of the guys knew of a great deal on a used but in-great-shape four-wheeler and he thought he'd mosey over to take a look at it. I told my cup of coffee that it was a ridiculous thought and a four-wheeler of any kind was out of the question. Ed's coffee argued back that I would be able to haul horse feed with ease, as well as accomplishing a million other odd jobs around the farm, making our lives so very much easier.

Agreeing that he should take a look at the machine to ease his mind and "get over it," I dismissed the subject and went on with my day.

I forgot about that morning and Ed's tire-kicking trip until about a week later when some pamphlets came in the mail with brand-new, shiny four-wheeler photos on the fronts. When confronted with the materials, Ed explained that he was real disappointed in all he had seen and heard about the used machines and just wanted to compare them to the new models. After some "friendly fire" in the kitchen, I was leaning a tish towards a handy-dandy new machine that would haul horse feed with a push of the thumb, but why fix what wasn't broke?

The southern drawl on the other end of the telephone was unmistakably sincere as the fellow explained that the new and improved next-year's model of four-wheeler would be ready to ship in a week's time. "ED!"

After a lengthy conversation and all but blaming the dog and the kitchen sink, Ed told his boots that, yes, he had bought a new four-wheeler but promised I would never have to lift or carry anything over ten pounds again on the farm.

Having the salesperson at the feed store carry and place my bags of feed in the trunk, I felt pretty as a princess knowing I wouldn't have to carry the bags to the barn when I got home. Pulling up to the shop, I saw there was no husband or four-wheeler in the yard — not even behind the third tree to the right.

Nick and Ray were milling about and, when asked where I might find my brand-spankin'-new feed hauler, they each pointed in different directions. About that time, Ed came pulling in with a mountain of pig feed on the back of the four-wheeler, parked it, got in his pickup, and left.

Carrying my feed bags to the barn, I pondered how big of a brand-new horse trailer I should purchase to haul a little pig feed...

Try This, Charlie

If Charlie Brown would let his hair down and tip over a few outhouses, maybe his Halloween would be a tish brighter each year. The meager little roundhead might have a better evening if he tried a few pranks, perhaps with a couple of aids, including a roll of toilet paper and an egg or two. Wouldn't that be a hoot if all the little darlings watching Charlie's yearly movie hugged and kissed their parents on the way out trick-or-treating, ammunition stuffed in their pockets?

Each year on this wonderful forgotten holiday that's lost in the rush before Thanksgiving and Christmas with just a side order of Pilgrim hats, I pray that a few past Halloween pranks stay in the past without resurrection or community notification.

A passed-down tradition, I would sure like to hear "the rest of the story" from my elders some day. Little segments of testimonials that have slowly been revealed through the years put my teenage shenanigans right to the top of the Statue of Liberty.

I would never, ever have thought to sneak onto my friend's farm in the middle of the night while they were sleeping, lead a pony from the barn, and place it in the entryway of their home! If I would have had the nerve, I at least would have been sure to remove the bushel basket of apples beside the door. When ponies overindulge on the little red appetizers, all heck sets loose… Dad lent a hand with the cleanup committee the next day, but I think Uncle Curt took all the blame.

Another meagerly mentioned prank heard between the lines from our elders was the year of the unreachable outhouse. Every farm had one, but this particular potty was smack dab in the center of town with lights all around and guarded with a shotgun from the owner's window the entire week of Halloween. Not coming right out and admitting his involvement in the toppling of the inaccessible outhouse, Dad used his friend Ted as an example one year after a few too many brews. He told how Ted had the plan laid out to a tee: a cable was attached to the back corner of the structure mid-October and strung through the back yards and along a creek on the way out of town, well hidden in the grass along the way. Sometime before dawn on Halloween night, Ted and his friends hooked the cable up to his pickup from across the creek and gave her hell. Dad laughed so hard each time he told the story, I'm still not sure how many small buildings were taken out, but the untouchable outhouse was toppled, along with half a city block. The crime scene was reported in the daily chronicle but Ted could never claim to be the champion toppler as there was a reward out for the foolish prankster.

I think us kids got pretty dang close to our traditional upbringing one year with a very well-placed, scary prank outside of town beside the cemetery. The dirt road was well traveled every night, but Halloween brought extra traffic with trick-or-treaters traveling from farm to farm. It took older brother half a day to climb the high-line pole with the rest of us assigned as lookouts. When a car would come from around the corner, we would yell to brother from our hiding spot in the ditch and he would hang hidden on the far side of the pole. I'm wondering if that's the reason he developed arthritis so bad in both arms as he got older. Anyway, big brother attached a pulley and wire to the top of the pole, and the other end was connected to a high tree branch in the middle of the graveyard. Swiping one of Mom's embroidered white sheets, we were all set after dark to scare the daylights out of trick-or-treaters as they drove past while our fake ghost flew by overhead.

It almost worked way too well; we laughed until we cried as cars fishtailed and sped around the corner when Casper came flying out of the cemetery right above them.

As we were deciding to wrap up our hilarious prank before someone called Ghostbusters, one last set of headlights rounded the corner. We pulled for all we were worth, still laughing hysterically, and the wire went "kaput" and broke apart directly over the pickup, floating Casper right down onto the windshield. Silence and dread followed as the truck hit the ditch.

Never in a million years could we be so lucky to hear Dad's tumble of swearing as he climbed out of the truck and promptly fell in the mud at the bottom of the ditch. Mom's lingo was never repeated by any of us as she opened the passenger door and dropped, high heels and all, into the murk.

Crawling on hands and knees through the grass and mud all the way home in the dark, the six of us made a pact to keep our little Halloween ghost episode silenced forever.

After Sunday school about a week later and before we sat down to pot roast, each of us kids said a silent prayer, as there on the guest chair sat a washed, ironed, and neatly folded Casper with Mom's stitched initials facing up...

Off the Farm

Ed stopped in the house the other day and asked if I needed anything in town and if I wanted to ride in with him. As he started to list off the places he was going, I thought, Oh, yay, I can really do some serious shopping at the truck equipment supply store. The next stop he mentioned was Fleet Farm; I was changed and in the pickup before Ed had found his wallet.

Fleet Farm is my "Rodeo Drive," sporting anything and everything a country gal could ever want or need. The last few years, when asked what was on my Christmas list, I just handed everyone a Fleet Farm catalog.

My mouth was watering as I thought of aisle one, where the greatest bags of old-fashioned candy are found—something the new superstores don't carry. Aisles six and nineteen had better be free of shoppers as Emily was on her way!

Driving down the interstate, we passed a semi trailer with the latest, greatest John Deere combine header loaded on the back. Ed had to slow down, speed up, and then slow down again to view every inch of the "green" thing as I studied my watch, musing over the five minutes of prime-time shopping I was losing.

Getting closer to "Christmas in July," we were stalled for a few minutes at an intersection as some goofball intending to take a turn decided at the last minute on "take-backs," unloading his cargo of pallets right onto the center of the intersection. I eyed the bits of scrap wood, thinking a helping hand could carry a few boards into the back of our pickup; Ed pushed the automatic door lock button for my side of the cab as he stared straight ahead.

With only one traffic light stalling us before my elbow-pushing shopping entrance, mentally I listed my first purchase as a watch without a second hand.

There was only a one-in-a-million chance from here to the Badlands that we could be stopped beside another pickup the exact same make and model as ours. Ed and the other fellow stared at each other while comparing their scratches and dents. I felt a lot better after glancing over and seeing the other wife studying her watch with her "mean face" turned on.

"Ed, the light's green! ED!"

At the truck equipment supply store, I waited in the pickup and wrote down my soon-to-be shopping selections on the corner of a feed sack. After aisle one I would mosey down the right side of the store, then go back for a second cart and hit the left side. When Ed's eyes were all agog at the full carts, I would remind him this was Fleet Farm and, of course, all the merchandise was farm-related. The items from aisles six and nineteen would be well hidden in the bottom of the carts.

Finally seeing the big orange and black sign ahead, my excitement drained as Ed slowed down by the Caterpillar machinery merchant. "Ed, ED, EDDDD, you're driving on the wrong side of the road!" In the corner of the lot there was apparently some type of new farming apparatus that he had never seen before. As the pickup automatically turned into the driveway, I gauged the distance, pondering if I could walk to Fleet Farm from there. Just a little too far and too much traffic to brave, I figured, and cursed the machine named after a bug.

"This will only take a minute," Ed said as he left me alone in the pickup to curse all things yellow.

Checking my watch again, I was horrified, realizing there would only be one hour of shopping bliss before Fleet Farm closed for the evening. Ed was analyzing every square inch of the Caterpillar thinga-majig and looking at it more lovingly than he did his firstborn son. I think he actually had tears in his eyes! My shopping bliss came to a crashing end when the salesman walked out of the building... Looking around in the cab for something to throw at him before he could get to Ed, I tore off my watch and aimed for a between-the-eyes hit, but it was too late—they had made eye contact.

At that moment, I knew exactly how the "Castaway" fellow felt as his volleyball floated away in the ocean. "I'm sorry, Fleet Farm, I'm sorry!"...

Lady Buggers

The Great Asian Beetle has won; I surrender and throw in the towel.

Introduced to this great country as a secret weapon to gobble up soybean-destroying aphids, the end result is "desperate housewives"!

I didn't notice the little buggers until a couple of years ago. Big deal, the farmer across the road had a mighty famous thousand-bushel-to-the-acre bean crop. What I didn't know was that, after the crop was harvested and their aphid lunch had disappeared, a zillion Asian beetles were heading across the road, up the driveway and right into my house!

Putzing around outside on a beautiful sunny September day, I was pulling weeds from around the horse barn when I noticed the big, white front door literally covered with ladybugs. Oh for nice, I thought, remembering how fun it was as a youngster to have the red, spotted darlings crawl around on your hand. But the instant that thought came, I was bitten, and then bitten again so hard that blood was drawn. Instantly, I was dive-bombed and munched on by a hundred of the "cute little ladybugs"! It was worse than the movie "The Birds" or even the ancient picture show where killer ants scoured the countryside, eating people alive.

Doing some digging around on the World Wide Web, I discovered and was totally devastated to find the actual culprit was the Asian beetle disguised as a ladybug. All childhood memories of play time with ladybugs were dashed and replaced with spots of torment. Surfing the Web further, I found it there in black and white: "Each Asian Beetle comes complete with no more and no less than 19 black spots on its wings." What the Web failed to say was the fact that they were born to agitate the heck out of any living being.

As I was enjoying a bowl of Captain Crunch Crunchberries the next morning, there she was, Lady Asian, crawling right up the side of the cereal box. Loitering all around the kitchen light were ten or fifteen of her sisters, ready to swoop down and finish off my last "berry." The toast popped up, and so did a charming little Asian from around the corner.

This was WAR! My personal space would not be taken over by the little red beasts! "Hear this, Asians: My home or anything close to me has never been falsely represented as an aphid and I deeply resent your intrusion!"

Now, I have a tish of imagination, but I swear I could see a couple of grins while little bitty teeth were self-sharpening.

Positioning the extension on the vacuum cleaner sideways, I was able to clear the ceiling of the little pests for the moment. I smiled as I walked out the door, having ended their little tea party.

Hup two three four, single file across the front counter as I was making supper, there they marched. Retrieving the vacuum, I found the odor inside from the previously collected red army was overwhelming. Another world-wide fact buried in the depths of information was that agitated Asians spurt out a batch of yellow stinky gunk for protection. Adding up the price of ten vacuum bags per day with no end in sight, I decided it was time for an emergency trip to the hardware store for Asian-beetle eliminators.

The salesman assured me that Pro-Trapper sticky glue traps would eliminate all bugs, no matter how many legs and spots they had or what part of the world they originated from. Guess what? Hup two three four, the next morning the bloodthirsty little varmints marched right around the sticky traps directly towards crunch and berry.

Back at the hardware store, I was handed "demon spray" and assured once again this can of "wonder squirt" would abolish all Asian beetles near and far. Reading the fine print at home, I discovered that, for best effect, I should spray each creepy crawler individually. Hmmm, a $20 can of spray snuffed out fifteen bugs and I could hear all their little friends laughing outside the door.

Mr. Hardware Salesman of the Year who didn't know his beetle juice from a hole in the ground saw me coming and placed a young innocent attendee behind the counter. "Ma'am, we have a Solo Backpack sprayer that easily enables you to fog around your home in no time at all, eliminating all Asian beetles, on sale for $89.99. The new and improved insecticide to use with this remarkable machine is also on sale for a mere $42.99." Receiving complimentary bug-proof rubber gloves and goggles, I was ready for my own "Little Big Horn."

My tulips tipped over, the red fern did not grow again, and the dog disappeared for two days, but all the ladybuggers were still alive and well.

Ed asked why I was digging up all the grass on the edge of the yard and why there were sacks of soybean seed stacked on the driveway. Defense and intelligence negotiation plan B was placed into effect as he was handed a spade and asked to help dig a bunker. Whistling "Dixie," I produced a jar of aphids that, when mixed with the growing soybeans, would stop the little ladies right in their tracks beside the white towel hanging from the flagpole…

Snow Angels

Ed called and said to leave town right away—the snow was coming down heavier and the wind was picking up. "OK, OK, just one more stop and I'll be on my way." In town, one doesn't see or realize the pickle a person can get into when heading out on the highway past the last protected building. From sixty mph to zero in one giant whiteout!

Putzing along at turtle speed, it was decision-making time: turn around or keep going? A quiet hotel, pizza delivery, and a TV remote all to myself sounded pretty darn good, but this time I kept on a-going as the chocolate cake mix in the grocery bag was screaming, "Get me home and bake me!" Two miles onto the highway, I was cussing myself for the bad decision. Hell was not rocks and fire; it was ice, snow, and wind!

This was by far not one of my best judgment calls, but I was supplied with a survival kit and a bag of Hershey bars. Thinking of Dorothy and the yellow brick road as the yellow lines slowly disappeared, I wondered how she would "click home" wearing a pair of Uggs. Teeny tiny little snowflakes were not going to get the best of Emily, but they were ganging up real fast and heading in a horizontal direction.

Bobbing my head sideways and then up, following the blowing snow, I wondered how many other fools were out and about, ready to be casualties of the evening. They say to keep your eyes on the road and not follow the snow. Whoever's bright idea that was must have been in a laboratory somewhere in Florida as it's pretty much automatic that after awhile your eyes, then your head, and then your car, are all going in the same direction. I was feeling a little alone, and it brought back memories of the time I was dumped off a horse in the middle of a 50-mile endurance ride with a 25-mile walk either way.

THUMP, thump, thump… I had either run over a sign, or a fellow fool who had run in the ditch or had a flat tire and was walking. Pulling off to the side of the road, I got out to inspect the situation with a "Whoa, it's an awfully cold and wicked place to be!"—and worried myself a tish when I looked down and saw the white lines in the middle of the highway. Not a good place to be when you're invisible to an oncoming semi. Figuring out that the thumps had been caused by pillow drifts across the road, I composed myself, scarfed down a Hershey bar, and headed out a little bit over to the right. Angry I had forgotten to grab the 12-pack of Coke from the trunk, I figured it probably didn't matter anyways as the freezing temperature, along with the car bucking over the drifts, was surely exploding the cans one by one.

"Can you hear me now?" was out of the question as cell phones and snowstorms don't mix. "The subscriber you are calling is unavailable." Excuse me? I was under the impression that cell phones were invented for emergencies, and by God, this was one of them! I made a note to contact customer service if I lived through the night and give them a piece of my boot.

Why don't we pay more attention to mile markers? I passed number 18; is that before or after my turn? Heck, I would probably end up in Alaska before the night was over. There's a farmstead not too far off the road that I should be able to see the yard light from, and then I could tell how far I had to go to turn onto our road. Between mile markers 19 and 20, I ate the whole bag of candy bars, deciding that if I was going to expire, it would be a blissful event.

Using the strap from my purse, I tied the passenger door open, and the seat belt held my handy-dandy emergency flashlight in perfect position to help me see the white line on the edge of the road. Heck, I was in good shape for traveling a max of 5 mph. The car was filling up fast with snow, but it needed a good washing anyways.

This was my turn; I could recognize the stop sign with the shotgun holes through it anywhere, even in a blinding snowstorm. I was home free! Three short miles to go and I would be pulling into our driveway.

I only had one problem: there are no white lines on gravel roads and the ditches were filled up with snow level with the road. Very thankful no one could see what I was doing, I held the driver's door open and used the ice scraper to poke on the road every few feet to feel solid ground. As I was driving east with a north wind, the snow blew right through the front seat along with my Hershey wrappers, most of the groceries, and my rear view mirror.

Just as I ran over our mailbox and saw the yard light, my cell phone chimed clear as a bell. Thankful for a human connection, I listened in disbelief as a telemarketer asked my views about global warming. "Now hear this!..." — and I buried him in the snow…

"Honey, I Shrunk the Barn"

August is a dandy month of the year. I particularly love the heat and humidity. They say the "harvest moon" is beautiful, but I've never seen it through the dust from the gravel roads and combines.

Directly after the last row of wheat is combined, we start baling straw. Oh, my most favorite job of all on the farm! I can only remember a handful of times the temperature was less than 95 degrees and without a threat of rain in the immediate forecast. It's always hurry up, get the baler out and greased, run to town for twine, and gather up as many neighbor kids as you can find to help stack bales.

A quick assessment of the operation would look like this: The smallest youngster drives the pickup while sitting on a cooler to see over the steering wheel while pulling a thirty-foot flat-bed trailer. Ed drives the tractor, and one of the older kids operates the Skid-Steer with a picker-upper that places eight bales at a time on the trailer. The rest of us are loading up stray bales, piling them on smaller trailers, in pickup boxes, and whatever has an area large enough to hold a straw bale or two. Eight to ten trips to the hayloft and two or three days later, we're finished for the year.

Rain was on the way, the sky to the west was dark, and thunder was echoing through the trees. Our crew resembled little ants, running around, tossing the last of the bales onto the trailer. Ed hurriedly removed the picker-upper from the Skid-Steer while saying, "Emily, quick, get in and drive this home before the storm hits."

"Huhhhh?" Now, just wait one minute, there's NO WAY I'm getting in that thing and driving down the road, much less trying to get it under cover! As I looked around for a replacement, the sinking "Honey, I need a pull" feeling made my skin crawl. The only relief-drivers left were too short to reach the foot pedals. "Can't we call someone?" That question didn't go over well as the rain was starting and Ed was about to take his hat off and stomp on it.

Crawling into the Skid-Steer, I made a quick mental assessment of my will and said goodbye to my limbs. Ed took eight seconds explaining that, to drive forward, you push the levers ahead; to slow down, stop, or reverse, you pull 'em back. "How do I turn?" fell on deaf ears as he was running to the tractor.

Oh, crap, it was now raining cats and dogs and I was in the lead in front of the tractor, an uncovered load of straw, and an assortment of vehicles. What happened over the next few minutes in the field put the Double Ferris Wheel to shame! Finally making it onto the road, I was soaked, and my hands kept slipping off the levers. When one lever was pulled and the other wasn't, the wicked machine took a diving turn toward the ditch. Trying to hang on and pulling back made the dang thing buck me right out of the seat.

How I made it to the yard I'll never know. Ed waved for me to put the Skid-Steer inside the barn... or at least that's what I thought. It wasn't until afterwards that I was told he was directing me toward the shop. It was raining so hard I could barely see him, and I thought "for dumb," why was I supposed to put the Skid-Steer in the barn? I only had about two inches on either side, but that's where I was told to go!

Making it in, my hand slipped off a lever and, "poof," a four-foot metal gate was taken out. As I over-corrected, the next casualty was a support beam. Thinking this was NOT a good situation and quickly planning my funeral, I tried to back out.

We now have a much larger front door to the barn. Ed eventually "got over it," but if I even mention in passing that we use the Skid-Steer, he runs and pulls the keys...

Resolution

This past New Year's, I figured it would be a good time to finally decide once and for all what I wanted to be when I grew up.

Thinking way back, I determined that being a "king weed puller" was not in the cards for me, just as it wasn't for my brothers and sisters when we were sent into a bean field with instructions to remove all king weeds, most of them wider around than little sister. Only the oldest brother was tall enough to see over the weed patches, and as he sat on his high throne blaring instructions to us shorter laborers, we snuck out of the field on our hands and knees, leaving dear big brother to deal with Dad and a zillion leftover king weeds. Big brother did not grow up to be an agronomist after he was fired and then ordered to clean the field by himself.

As a young horse trainer's assistant, I told everyone and the moon that a horse trainer was surely what I wanted to be when I grew up. Since I was made up mostly of legs at that age, my mentor worded it very carefully that I was light and agile enough to be promoted to "first rider of colts." Not knowing any better and having a very sketchy job description, I disqualified myself after being tossed over the moon more times than I cared for. I still list "horse trainer" on my resume; in fact, just yesterday I taught my old grey gelding to actually act like a horse.

Dog catching was a *maybe*-foreseeable occupation. They said I was the best of the best at luring all stray, street-bound dogs to my official yellow pickup truck in no time at all. Given clearance to the city, along with a two-way radio, I would drive by motorists and pretend to be taking a very serious call from Captain Adam 12 himself. My career-ending event had to do with a lab/setter cross that could spot my yellow truck from a mile away when he was cruisin' the neighborhood. Time after time, that mutt would evade my alley traps and nets, loping off with a grin on his face and a fake bandana around his neck.

Now, the pet-store stint was the mother of all jobs, and the only one I was ever fired from. Buddy was his name and he lounged in a glassed-front cubicle overseeing his little jungle of fish, rodents, and reptiles. One of my assignments was to shine up the front of Buddy's dwelling before the store opened so everyone that wandered by could clearly see the beautiful, well-behaved little monkey and perhaps take him home. Buddy and I didn't get along too well from the beginning, and as time went on, he took great pains to make my job pure hell. After each cleaning of his glassed-front home, the little varmint dug in his nose and flicked boogers all over the inside of the glass and then pooched his lips at me in an insulting kiss. Buddy would also make sure the store owner wasn't watching and then moon me any chance he got. The cake topper was the day I was cleaning behind Buddy's wire-backed cage and got a little too close to his domain. That cute little monkey grabbed my hair and pulled me in like a fish on a reel. Held in a death trap, I didn't dare reach up with my hands or they would be amputated along with what was left of my hair. The only weapon in reach was the broom, and the handle fit perfectly between the wire mesh, giving me one chance in ten of survival. Just as I slid the broom into the cage to back the monkey off, the store owner came around the corner to see what the commotion was about. Buddy instantly released his grip, sat back with his hands up in the air, howling for all he was worth, and I was released of my duties for attempted murder of a defenseless monkey.

I think everyone at one time or another has wanted to be a professional photographer. Being no exception to the rule, I've shot a few really good Kodak moments on my way to imminent stardom. Way too impatient for shutter speeds or zoom dimensions, I think a master's degree in Polaroid-camera use should be sufficient.

Just last Saturday as the Lifetime Channel had consumed my very soul, Ed called in a frantic voice, saying he needed my immediate help with a National Geographic photography session. Rolling my eyes and saying goodbye to Lifetime, I hoped this shoot would be a bit more interesting than the last one of an owl in the barn. Yep, an owl in the barn was the cause for my frostbite and midnight romp of photography.

Hopping in the pickup with camera ready, I asked Ed just what was so photogenic that I had to go out in twenty-below temperatures. Driving the truck like it was a snowmobile, he "shushed" me as we snuck up on the subject. Now, how was asking a quiet question in a one-ton truck with the motor grinding going to scare away the subject?

Pointing to the middle of a field while turning the corner, Ed whispered, "Hurry, shoot the picture!" Well, there was a whole lot of snow and this would be one great white photo, but what the heck was I taking a picture of? Zooming in on a blob of brown— oh, come on, no way was I going to take a photo of two foxes on a "date"!

Maybe next year I'll decide what I want to be when I grow up. Heck, I might even take a writing class and become a featured columnist…

Calamity Janes

Who wouldn't jump at the chance to put the first few miles on a brand new pickup?

Ed had made the transaction and the dealership was waiting for his trade with the new truck's keys all shined up and ready to hand over. Dang, a little harvest problem had gotten in his way and I was asked to make the trip. Aw shucks, there was gardening to do and critters to take care of, but I supposed the time could be arranged to mosey on down the road to collect up his new pickup. I thought the hand-on-the-Bible thing was a bit much but Ed insisted, and I swore to bring the new truck home in showroom condition.

Brandy! Drop whatever you're doing and grab your wallet! We're going on a road trip to pick up Ed's new truck and there's a great new western store right down the block from the dealership!

In no time at all, Brandy and I were listening to the long version of "Ride, Cowboy, Ride" while bouncing down the highway in Ed's old truck. There was friendly silence for a while as we both wondered if the dealership had actually seen the replacement trade that was on the way, but we figured it was a done deal as Ed never, ever sent me on one of his buying trips, least of all for a new truck.

The disgusted looks from fellow travelers at the rest stop made both Brandy and me a little uncomfortable, but as we filled the smoking radiator with water, we snickered, knowing the return trip to the same stop would bring stares of admiration and awe when we climbed out of the sassy new truck for a little sip of water from the fountain.

The suit-and-tie fellow hurried out of the dealership with a fire extinguisher as we pulled up, but when handed the paperwork, he wiped his forehead with a neatly folded, white hankie and motioned a lot worker to place the bubbling truck "way out back." There was friendly silence between Brandy and me as the worker pushed the old pickup around the corner and we bid farewell.

Holy cow, the amazing new truck had working air conditioning and double cup holders, and the words to our "Ride, Cowboy, Ride" CD sang out clear as a bell! Just one sonata later, we pulled up to the new western-wear store, ready for some heavy-duty shopping. I suggested to Brandy that it might be a good idea to wrap some tape around the metal stirrups of her newly purchased saddle before she tossed it in the pickup box, but, oh no, she was in a hurry to get back in the store for our two boxes of boots.

There was friendly silence for a while as we covered the scratch with mascara.

The Taco John's order was delayed a bit as the voice on the other side of the microphone asked us to roll up our lariats and turn the volume down. Thinking the young fellow at the ordering window was a little too big for his britches and needed a lesson in proper pickup music, I handed Brandy her soda as the attendant and I had a little stare-down. Brandy's eyes were fixed on her new saddle in the pickup box and down went the soda, soaking the center console and most of the seat. Asking for extra napkins and receiving an "I told you so" gaze from the Proactive-wearing server, we wiped up the stains as best we could in a bit of friendly silence.

I'm sure the bird "had to go," but he sure didn't have to go that much, as the whole side of the shiny new, black truck was streaked in white while we rolled down the freeway. Brandy's extra-hot-sauce container spilled all over the floor as she leaned out the window, telling me how much bird poop was on the right-hand side of the box. We drove in friendly silence for a while.

Pulling into the rest stop for what was supposed to be our "hey, look at us *now*!" return, I grabbed the hose from the hydrant and Brandy removed the plastic from around my new curry brush to clean off the truck. Awhile later, in friendly silence we both read the brush's label stating it contained fifty percent steel.

Taking a short cut home to see a friend's new foal crop in the pasture, the "No winter maintenance" sign should have also stated, "No summer driving after rain." After walking to our friend's house to borrow a tractor, there was no way to get back in the pickup without spreading the entire interior with mud. After a little silence, we both perked up as the mud covered the little swirly brush scratches along the entire box side.

Ready to wear new boots, brush our horses, and try out the new saddle, we turned up the ol' "Ride, Cowboy, Ride" music for a little sing-along the last few miles. We knew the jackrabbit didn't mean to jump out in front of the truck and try to outrun us, but the little bugger could have slowed down a bit instead of kicking up rocks at the windshield. After some friendly silence, both Brandy and I agreed the big crack resembled a horse's eye and the little ones were similar to Charlotte's web-home.

Ed stood in total silence as we crawled out of his new pickup, loudly singing, "Run, Cowgirls, Run," and hightailing it for the barn...

The Color Purple

I was tickled pink to be invited to lead the Fourth of July parade with my then barely-out-of-kindergarten, four-year-old, white gelding. Goose came with the name, and it didn't take long at all to figure out why. In horse talk, "goose" means "a little spooked" by just about anything that makes a sound, moves, or may move sometime in the future. Too naive to know any better, I happily accepted the parade position without a second thought that Goose might not be up to it.

Preparing for the spectacular event took a little bit of time and patience as both Goose and I had to look our best as we traveled down Main Street with crowds applauding and cameras flashing.

The sparkle kit for horses didn't come with directions. First testing it out on a watered-down Holstein cow, I found that the red and blue sparkles held well to the hair, but then blended into a bluish purple. The angry Holstein bull did not appreciate sparkles sprinkled within ten feet of him, and I had to give up cow-testing real quick before both the sparkle bottle and I were tossed over the fence.

The white goat took to sparkles real quick—too quick, in fact, as he pooped purple for a week—but not before I figured out that rubbing the mixture against the hair grain was a brilliant solution. Goose would be leading the parade with his legs matching the flag.

Packaged in extravagant wrappings, my red, white, and blue outfit came in the mail straight from the Acme Parade Clothing Co. Nothing against the Acme Co., but they must be very little people as the one-size-fits-all blue tights were just a tish snug. The red and white striped shirt fit OK, but for the life of me, I couldn't figure out if the square piece of material with stars on it was supposed to be a bandana for me or a saddle blanket for the horse.

It was suggested that I wear plenty of makeup to present the parade in proper fashion. Going with the natural look all my life, I had a bit of a problem applying the eyeliner and false eyelashes the morning of the big event. The directions didn't say anything about eyelash glue or the eyeliner being semi-permanent. Rocky the Raccoon would have looked very pale in the mirror next to me, as no amount of Ivory soap would remove the black circles. Loose face powder was applied with a fancy applicator, and when I sneezed into the container, a thin layer was also applied to my hair, the mirror, and the rest of the room. Spending a little time powder finger-painting on the counter eased my mood a bit.

Backing out of the trailer at the parade site, Goose took one look at the commotion and hopped right back in. With a little coaxing, he was out and saddled in plenty of time, and we were both sparkling and dressed to the hilt for our debut down Main Street.

Then Goose caught a glimpse of the fellow in the white coat carrying the flag toward us, spun around, and dumped me right out of the saddle. By the time the band started playing, Goose and I had come to an understanding that the flag was not going to eat him, and we were ready to move forward.

Goose's ears perked up and then laid flat back as, dead ahead, was a collection of Shriners driving straight toward us and doing wheelies in their mini-cars. Holy Hannah, was I ever in a pickle, and the Shriners didn't have a clue they were about to be totaled out by a terrified white horse! The spin-and-dump thing was getting a little old, but the fellow wearing the white coat helped me up off the pavement for the second time and saved the day when he ticketed the little cars to the end of the line. Humpty Dumpty couldn't have said it better as the cymbals in the band crashed at the end of their song, and everyone cheered as Goose walked straight down the middle of the street on his hind legs.

Through my embarrassed tears, the semi-permanent eye makeup picked a fine time to let loose, and my peripheral vision caught the corner of a false eyelash beautifying my cheek.

At the end of the parade, the black eyeliner, combined with red lipstick and blue sparkles, made my face look like one giant purple lollipop. I made a mental note to write stern letters to the Ivory soap company, the Acme Clothing people, and the "falsely represented" false eyelash corporation.

I was thirsty as all get-out at the finish area, and a soda was offered by the man in the white coat. As I sipped the grape Shasta, the clown with the giant green hair thought he would walk up to pet the pretty white horse. Goose saw lunch, and the clown had no clue that his glued-on wig was about to become a horse snack.

I was purple, the clown's bare head was purple, and the helpful parade attendant now sported a suit jacket the color of grape Shasta. About that time, the festivity planners directly behind us by the grandstands started testing the fireworks for later that evening. Talk about a blur of purple...

Good Morning, Wilbur

It's 5:00 on a Sunday morning; do you know where your sleep is? How about your pigs? Ed and I can sleep right through a porcine escape from Alcatraz, but the friendly neighbor isn't too friendly any longer when his garden of sweet corn is being eaten to smithereens by a whole bunch of hogs at daybreak. I sure can't figure out how he heard them; the whole group arrived pretty much in single file with only daffodils and Butter Kernel on their minds.

Phone calls at any time during the wee hours immediately get one's guard up, even though you try to explain to the caller, "Yes, I was awake; I really was."

Apologizing profusely on the phone, we scrambled for herding supplies. I took the pickup and the dog while Ed flew past on the four-wheeler. "Green Acres" was green no more as we came on the scene and surveyed the damage. The fit-to-be-tied neighbor was standing guard over his wife's flower garden, trying to wave the hogs away with the end of a garden hose. Mrs. Neighbor was screaming directions to her better half from out the window while holding her nose. Both Ed and I got the chuckles as her directions sounded more like a hog snort than what an actual hog could do.

Promising to replace the sod and replant their flowers, I let the dog out with the magic words "sic 'em." Dog sicced one hog and then let out a howl that woke the entire neighboring county as Queen Tabby Cat of the neighbors' farm sicced our dog. Tail tucked and out of there in a flash, he left us dogless and helpless to round up the escapees.

There's usually one mean old lead sow that stands out and promises the rest of the herd greener grass on the other side. If we found her and got her smelly rump moving towards home, the rest would follow with a little coaxing. That morning we couldn't pick her out as the whole lot was circling around Mrs. Neighbor's daisy garden like vultures on road kill. As we were trying to decide on either Plan A, which would take the herd back home down the road, or Plan B, going through the wheat field, the old lead sow ran right by us in a tizzy with Terror Tabby close behind. Totally embarrassed that our dog was outdone by a simple feline, we more or less followed the herd into the wheat field and Plan B took effect by default.

Dead furrows — there's a reason they call them that, and Plan B came to a sliding stop as lead sow hit the first one and decided to stop, drop, and roll in the tidy drainage ditch in the middle of the field. Spreading out like a wave, the whole dang group flopped around in the mud as the sun was now up, along with the temperature.

Taking a break, I started scraping the gunk off my boots with the shoo stick as Ed came flying up on the four-wheeler, questioning my herding abilities without a word — just "the look." I ducked down in the wheat and covered my mouth so Ed couldn't hear me laughing as he had spun around with the four-wheeler, hitting the dead furrow with a very dead ending. As I was within forty miles, I accepted responsibility for his little accident. We were now not only dogless but also on foot for the rest of the roundup.

The smell was horrendous, and in the three-foot-tall wheat we had no idea where or what direction the skunk was heading. Pigs are supposed to have a great sense of smell and should have hightailed it straight for home, but, oh, no, they lollygagged around in circles, making us both decide porcine did not have much for brains — never mind that the Farmer's Almanac said they did.

With the sun at about 10:00 and both of us completely worn out, the roundup was close to an end at the fifty-yard line from the barn. Dog must have decided he had cowered long enough from his run-in with Tabby the Terrible and trotted out to help just as lead sow was stepping inside the barn. Ed and I sat in the shade and watched as the genius farm dog chased the whole herd out the driveway and down the road...

Color Blind

It was one of those delightful summer mornings. By seven, the thermometer read ninety-nine in the shade while the happy TV weatherman should have been strung up the nearest tower after stating what a beautiful day it would be.

Sipping coffee with an ice cube chaser, I paused in my skimming through the newspaper and asked Ed how we might spend a nice little chunk of extra cash. Rereading the article to clarify what my lottery winnings would add up to, I noticed another write-up telling that, at the local county fair, a contest for the hardest water in the area was being held by a local water-softener company. The winner would receive a lump sum of $300, and I immediately daydreamed through the aisles of Herberger's, deciding what to buy with my half of the loot.

Years earlier the well had run dry on the farm, and without delay, another one had to be dug. They came with a huge truck and drilled pipe after pipe into the ground. A hundred feet, then two hundred, then three. No water or even oil could be coaxed to the surface. The chairman of the cattywampus operation ordered more pipe, and down they went again, to four hundred feet, then five. Ed and I were told they would have to relocate to a new spot and the price would be double for them to start over. I've always been pleased as punch that Ed told the crew to first try another fifty feet down. The well drillers spit out their snoose and tipped over their beverage cans as the water gushed a hundred feet in the air from five hundred and forty nine feet below. We had more water than anyone could ever have dreamed of, and the foreman yelled, "Cap it! This job is completed!"

One teeny tiny little detail was left out; no one bothered to test the water for hardness.

About a week later, I noticed a carroty-colored tint to my hair, the dish towels were a shade of burnt sienna, and the toilet bowl had a rosy-orange ring around the inside. The water was hard as a rock. I could almost stand Ed's socks up in place after washing them, but he didn't mind; they were easier to put on.

Complaints were hopeless as "We have water, don't we?" was repeated over and over.

At the time, I had a white horse, and before a local show, the required bath was given. I will never forget the comments and rude stares at that horse show as my sweet little white horse was branded as half zebra.

There was only one thing left to do as far as I was concerned, and that was to drill a new well. Putting my plan of attack into action, I bought a container of orange dye and sprinkled "just a bit" in the mud hole that the pigs lounged in. A hose fed the mud hole from the amazing gushing well and, boy, did I sleep with a huge smirk on my face that night.

Raising Yorkshires, a breed of pure white pigs, Ed about had a heart attack when he went out to feed the next morning and observed a pen full of Durocs, a predominant breed of "red" colored pigs. Mad as a wet hen, Ed thought it was the water in the mud hole that had caused his pigs to turn into incredible edible strawberry shortcakes. My plan had worked perfectly!

A new well was promptly ordered from a different company, and everyone was happy ever after as the water tested perfectly soft and clean.

We kept the "gusher" well in working order for fire disasters, and that's where I drew the water from to claim our winnings.

By the time I arrived at the fairgrounds, my water sample had turned a deep dark orange, and the smiley water-softener agent about fainted dead away as I held out my hand for the cash. In a scurry of activity behind the counter, the suited-up agents tested my sample over and over again. Mr. Shawn Higgins from the State Department of Health was called in to do a final test and, while gawking at the sample, asked, "Do you people actually drink this water?" Dang!—to this day I wish I would have put on a red wig, decorated my teeth with orange lipstick, and asked Mr. Higgins to kick my shin as it was hard as iron...

Techno-Drama

Years and years ago, Dad was talking to a machinery dealer, asking for a price on a new digger, and the salesman told him he would send a list of his current inventory via e-mail and asked for Dad's address. I don't think I've ever seen Dad so mad as he slammed the phone down, saying, "What's next—tractors that drive themselves?"

Last week, I discovered just how true his words would be. When talking to Aunt Helen, who was on her cell phone, I could hear Uncle Curt say, "Thanks for the paper," with an idling tractor noise in the background. When I asked what was up, she explained that Uncle Curt sat back and read the paper while the tractor's GPS escorted him straight as an arrow up and down the field by itself. All Uncle Curt had to do was mark his page and steer around at the ends. What next?—program them from home while the farmer sits in his recliner?

I program my cell phone to vibrate and high ring tone; if I can't hear the dang thing, I see it trying to jump out of my purse or dance around on the table, or I can feel it trying to escape my back pocket.

You all know how much Emily enjoys the sight of a wood tick. Last week, one of the little creepy crawlers was spotted on my sleeve, and I ran to and fro around the house like a mad woman! While I was brushing the little creepy crawler off into the sink, the cell phone rang from my back pocket… Not very good timing for a vibrating phone and a woman being attacked by a wood tick, as both were flushed down the toilet at the same time. I guess "can you hear me now?" was out of the question.

Heading to town for a new phone, I felt totally alone and withdrawn from society. What if Ed needed some parts?—how would he contact me? What if, what if, what if? After a while, I felt kind of free, and awhile after that, I figured a little side trip to Herberger's would be awesome as no one in the whole wide world would know my whereabouts or could interrupt a serious meeting with Sir Calvin Klein.

Following the line of cars turning at the detour sign, I somehow ended up alone in a nice neighborhood at a four-way stop in front of a young man holding a "Stop for Street Workers" sign. Ordinarily, this would have put me right through the roof and the local congressman would have been called, but he lucked out as my mode of communication was in the dunk along with the creepy crawler. Ignoring the street worker's wave to move on, I had spotted the eighth world wonder and was too fascinated to drive anywhere.

On the lawn beside me was a little round machine about ten inches high sporting the logo of Robo Mower. I had heard these little mowing wonders existed, but figured only kings and royalty had access to them.

Holding my breath as little Robo buzzed along straight toward the street, I figured he would be road kill in no time at all. Precisely at the edge of the lawn the little machine executed a perfect U-turn, and back the other way he went without missing a blade of grass. Reaching into my purse to call Ed to tell of my amazing find, I silently cursed little Woody and the flushing episode. Calvin and his accessories would have to be put on hold for awhile as this demonstration of amazing technology was by far a better buy.

I wished I had brought some lunch along because Robo had just about finished the lawn and I wasn't going anywhere, betting myself he would crack a beer and park in the shade after the last round. About that time, a huge Irish setter trotted from around the corner of the house and followed Robo, nosing the machine's rear. Rehearsing my speech to Ed about what I had discovered, I had to memorize in a hurry as Irish walked over to the last un-mowed part of the turf and took a dump. Forgetting the "beer bet," I upped the ante, thinking Robo may have a pooper scooper up his sleeve. As Robo approached the dump, he stopped, circled in place for a bit, and then backed up and rolled over on his side. I guessed the techno inventors didn't own dogs or hadn't looked that far ahead, and I wondered what Robo's reaction would be if placed in our cow pasture.

Thoroughly disappointed in Robo's demonstration, I fired up the old Buick to find my way through the maze of detours. A commercial on the radio caught my interest: iRobot was on sale at the local housewares store for an incredible discount. The sales pitch stated that the little round genie could be let loose in one's home and all the floors would be spotless forever after.

Thinking iRob must be a sissy cousin to Robo the Lawn Whiz, I wondered what the little machine would do if he came across a spider while polishing the kitchen floor. I bet myself a twelve pack that little iRob would scream bloody murder, rotate in a circle moving off toward the bathroom, and flush himself down the toilet…

Smokey the Bear

Turning onto our gravel road from the highway, I saw there was a little foreign-looking car parked smack dab in the middle about half-ways to our farm. Any car parked on our road is considered suspicious as the road is basically a dead end and you'd have to be nuts to want to go there most days.

Slowing down, I was ready to pounce on the stranger when a lady jumped out and started flailing her arms and screaming at me that I would be burnt alive if I drove any further. Thinking "cult" or worse, I eyed up a speedy three-point turnaround as the woman approached my car.

"I've called the fire department and am blocking the traffic so no one will be harmed," said the woman. I eyed the smoldering cornfield and realized the poor gal must have led a secluded city life, as she obviously had never come across a field being burned on purpose. I got the giggles and imagined what the gal would think if she was ever in the middle of one of our "real fire" catastrophes.

Every farm kid burns a barn down, right?

According to Dad, it wasn't on the "smart things to do list" for children to use authentic candles in a stall while practicing for the Sunday school nativity play, and we were grounded for life. Grandma spilled the beans a while later, and Dad had to set us free after we found out he had burned down not one but two barns as a youngster.

Hauling horse muck to a pile behind the barn and burning it is a normal, everyday activity. Not so normal is when the fire spreads to the surrounding dry grass and threatens to burn half the farm down. When this happens more than once during a week's time and Ed is called in off the tractor to help put out burning horse poop, aggravated hat-stomping and the words "glue factory" are used.

One spring after a huge rain, my shins were totally black and blue after the wheelbarrow kept making an abrupt halt in the mud on the way to the manure pile. With a few well-shod horses in the corral next to the barn, the ground was soon packed down enough to make a fresh muck pile in the midst of it. Not thinking, I lit the pile on fire and went back to the barn for another load. Old Nellie must have had an internal death wish as she lay down and rolled next to the burning heap, catching her tail on fire. "Stop, drop, and roll" doesn't work with a thousand-pound horse, but a well-aimed garden hose saved the day. Nellie's name turned to "Stumpy" after that little incident, and I kept her well-hidden until her tail grew back.

Bottle-rocket wars were the highlight of every Fourth of July until the neighbor kid built his combat dugout next to Dad's straw stack. Our entire ammunition dump was confiscated, and it took us kids a week to rake up the burnt straw.

Every family has a "firebug" and ours is no exception. On the first official day of fall, rain or shine, Uncle Curt is out burning anything he can reach with a torch from the four-wheeler: cornfields, ditches, thick grass around the culverts, and anything else that looks like it may cause a hindrance for the upcoming winter's blowing snow.

It took seven summers of hoeing our shelterbelt of newly planted trees before they finally produced enough foliage to catch the wind and snow. I got a little nervous when Uncle Curt made a drive-by in the morning and again that afternoon, slowing down by the corner next to our trees. Peeking out the side window of the house, I kept a close eye on him, and dang if he didn't drive right through a nice stand of dry ditch grass and onto the edge of the combined cornfield, aiming his torch.

With just a little breeze blowing in the opposite direction, I didn't worry too much as Ol' Smokey did his little fire dance and ignited the cornstalks.

I went about my business and semi-forgot the burning field until Uncle Curt came flying in on his four-wheeler, plowing straight through the small trees, over the lawn and up the front steps of the house. Yelling "Fire, Fire!" and pointing toward the field was about all Uncle Curt had left in him. "Holy Moly!" and 911 was all I could comprehend as over the top of the trees I spotted an enormous inferno!

Panicked and trying to dial for help with the television remote, I don't remember talking to anyone, especially the gal that kept insisting on an actual address instead of "five miles east and one mile north" of the nearest town.

The neighbors had seen Uncle Curt's giant smoke signals and were there to help an hour before the local F Troop of volunteer firefighters showed up. Apparently, the official fire assistants were busy with their annual search-and-destroy Miller Light party, and all had left their beepers behind.

Exhausted after the last ash was stomped out with only a few trees lost, we all had a great tale to tell for years to come. Captain Yogi and his sidekick BooBoo would be the first chapter each time as they had parked their volunteer fire truck close to the north trees for safety... the ones that had burned up...

"Dear Mom..."

Dear Mom,

Sorry it's taken me so long to write back to you. Thank you very much for the anniversary card. I can't believe it's been a whole year already!

Everything's well here; the crops are in and the livestock are all healthy.

We had a litter of sixteen pigs last week; Ed's trying to keep the runts alive to set the record for the county. Two of them are in the warmest corner of the kitchen in a box, and we're bottle-feeding them every three hours. The house cat is a little miffed; she pooped in their box.

We finally put a clothesline up and it's working well except for the goat chewing the bottoms off two pair of Ed's jeans. We can't afford to buy new ones, so I told Ed to just tuck what was left into his boots. The clothesline is now a foot taller.

Fried chicken was on the list for supper the other night, but for as many times as you showed me the proper way to cut one up, I just can't seem to do it right. I ended up with three breasts, one leg, and a bunch of square parts. I threw the whole thing in a pot and made soup instead. It was pretty good, except the noodles kept sticking to the bones.

We sorted calves yesterday, and everything was going great until the dog came running around the corner of the barn chasing the old tomcat and spooked the whole herd. The cattle took out the electric barbed-wire fence and scattered all over the place. After we got them rounded up, Ed went to fix the fence and forgot it was still plugged in. Holy smokes, did he ever let out a spiel when one of the barbs got caught on his shirt and he turned the wrong way, wrapping the fence around himself. I think he glowed in the dark the entire night!

You would be proud of me; I planted my very first garden! The seeds got a little mixed up when I tipped the pail over as the fire truck was arriving to put out the grass fire that spread from the burning manure pile. Can sweet corn grow in the same row as tomatoes?

Our new neighbors stopped by the other evening for a visit. They both seem to be very nice but didn't stay too long. I'm wondering if Harley didn't have something to do with it. If I forgot to tell you about Harley, he's a goose that some jokester put in our trailer the last time we hauled cattle to the stockyards. Harley likes to sneak up from behind and bite the rump of anything that walks. One day, he took a chunk out of the dog while it was sleeping. I saw it happen from the kitchen window and laughed for an hour as Harley hopped on top of a fence post, smirking at the dog trying to eat through the post to get the goose down.

Anyway, Harley snuck up behind the neighbor gal when we were standing there visiting and bit her pretty good. When she yipped and turned around to see what had bit her, Harley was already taking a chunk out of her husband's rump. We got some dirty looks as they drove off, but they did agree to come over next Sunday after church for pot roast.

An irritating fellow down the road has learned to fly an airplane. He must not sleep very well as every morning at the break of dawn he was swooping his plane right over our house. Ed got mad and went up on the barn roof with a can of spray paint. I didn't ask him what he wrote, but the neighbor now flies way around our farm.

Tell Dad I changed a flat tire on the pickup all by myself for the very first time! Ed was a little mad at the three holes in the box where the jack went through on my first tries, but I figured out the right place to put it and "whalaaa," I can now drive down the road and help anyone in distress with a flat.

Hope all is well and write when you can…

Love, Emily

Necessities

How many times do I have to find where I stashed it and then drag out my winter attire again? This up-and-down, in-and-out spring weather has gotten me flabbergasted.

Two weeks ago, the breeze was from the south and the snow was gone. I could feel the dandelions squirming around in the grass, ready to sprout. In the back closet I traded my Carhartts, Sorrels, and bomber hat for a hooded sweatshirt, rubber boots, and baseball cap.

I unplugged the water tank heater, neatly packing it away in the box that says "winter," and rolled the hose out to the outside hydrant. The extension cords for the vehicles were nicely wrapped up and hung on the treadmill that's conveniently located in the corner of the garage. The "Frosty the Snowman" yard ornament was tossed; he had had a very bad winter.

Then — poof! — a foot of snow and record-setting low temperatures. The water tank heater was unpacked and sat nicely on top of the ice, melting a cool little circle underneath. I wore my Carhart coat over the hooded sweatshirt, and the frozen hose broke in half when I tried to roll it up, but I wouldn't give up my rubber boots! No, siree, once those marvelous water- and mud-treaders were unpacked, they stayed out for the season.

Three pairs of socks made the easy slip-ons nicely winterized while omitting a pair every day or two as the temperatures rose. I LOVE my rubber boots; easy on, easy off, they don't shrink, and they don't stretch out. If the insides get a little wet when walking through a puddle you thought was a tish shallower, plastic bag liners are available with most grocery purchases.

One thing you can't do with rubber boots, and that I caution others about, is kicking. Kicking a frozen steel gate to get it loose is just plain brainless, unless you have a husband nearby to blame. Big-black-toe phobia lasts for a very long time.

Another foolish thing to try while wearing rubber boots is attempting to run. A person can sprint right over themselves twice in ten giant leaps while closely resembling a duck with three feet.

When the water puddles dry up but the mud is still deep, rubber boots are a little challenging, kind of like trudging with a toddler hanging onto each ankle. Not to despair, though; the mud is easily kicked off but, way too often, the boot goes right with it. At this point, remind yourself to be closer to dry ground the next time, as it doesn't work too well hopping one-footed in mud.

I Googled "rubber boots" once to get a bit of history and guess what? If Charles Ingalls (Pa from "Little House on the Prairie") would have lived thirty years longer, he too could have had the easy life, wearing rubber boots. To think that this wonderful footwear has been around since the late 1800s is creepy. Charles would turn over in his grave if he could see what's become of them, though.

Pink flowered, stripes, poka dots, sissy pull on-straps, and I've even seen them with a heel! Those fancy-pants designers in New York are putting a bad rap on the most required footwear accessory of the farm. Rubber boots were invented, and intended to stay, black!

I could buy a purple couch or a new horse and Ed wouldn't notice, but the instant I walked out of the house in a new pair of black rubber boots, I would get the "Were those necessary?" look.

Farm gals just can't have enough pairs of black rubber boots…

Party On

Thank goodness the month of March is over: Celebrating National Agriculture Month just about did me in with all the festivities and party favors!

I'm just wondering, when did all this merriment come into play? Whose bright idea was it to have a party each and every day for a whole month to celebrate pitching poop, milking cows, or getting stuck in the mud with a tractor?

OK, OK, I may have a bit of an defensive attitude when it comes to getting stinky or covered in dirt, but, seriously, just what on God's green earth were we supposed to be carrying on about until three in the morning for a solid thirty days?

I suppose "green" is the key word to celebrate feeding the world as it's the color of plants as they sprout, but then the crops dry up to an ugly brown so harvesting can be done. I'm not too sure, but wouldn't the brown harvest be considered more like Thanksgiving, and we could "party on" for one day in the fall instead of the thirty days it takes for this new extended holiday?

To me, green would be the color of my face as I tried to back a four-wheeled anhydrous tank out of the way of a semi at the elevator as the truck driver stood with crossed arms, spitting snoose on my tires.

A purplish shade of green would sum it up well when I was told to drop off the tank at Loopy's 80. You see, all the trucks, combines, and fields in the family have nicknames, and if you're not smart enough to put the name to the place or thing the first time around, you're screwed. It would be beyond all reason for someone to say, "Take the first left at 190th Avenue and then drop the tank in the second field road to the right." Oh no, it's "Hop in George, hook up the pot, and drop it off at the river bend field."

Celebrating a little older and greener, a decayed, well-past-prime goose egg has a burnt-cinnamon tinge of brownish green to it and, when well aimed, can take down a young sibling with only the smell.

Dad was green for a whole month one time. I bet he was the one who started this thirty-day, wondrous celebration out of plain old spite over his bad luck one day.

Little brother had graduated from using the Sears and Roebuck catalog under his rump to see over the steering wheel, and we all know at that age every farm kid receives their license. After proudly transporting lunch out to the field, his license was suspended indefinitely due to the little incident between the hood of the pickup and the tail end of the combine.

Dad's face turned a dark shade of lime green when oldest brother, pulling a huge load of silage with a tractor that afternoon, turned a tish too short out of the field approach and tipped the entire operation over in the steep ditch.

Later that day, the big bin holding most of Dad's harvested wheat started to creak and groan. Lo and behold if the whole darned thing didn't split wide open to unveil the world's largest bird feeder.

Dad was colored to a military shade of green by nightfall when he went to feed the cattle and there were none to be found. "Gate" was not a nickname but a word very often forgotten after the phrase "close the." It was a very long night trying to locate fifty Black Angus cows with no moon and one flashlight.

Back to the moment and on second thought, perhaps all farmers and ranchers should extend the thirty-day happy hour to having a birthday party each and every time an animal is born. Could you imagine what the price of wheat would be for the flour to make all those birthday cakes? Sugar beets would have to be guarded twenty-four hours a day to sweeten the cakes, and soybean oil would bring $50 a barrel.

Thinking a little more outside the box, every blade of wheat that sprouted would necessitate a happy dance, and boots would wear out pretty dang quick, thus placing leather (cows) at a few hundred bucks a pound.

Chickens would be laying golden eggs at a hundred bucks a pop, and sheep would be running for their lives, protecting their wool from the festival clothing designers. Party animals—now that's a new thought…

Treasure Hunt

Another Easter is past with the kids too old for egg hunting and grand-kids too young. Taking a break for a couple of years won't bother me any, as just last month the dog came trotting up with a pastel plastic egg filled with melted chocolate and covered in layers of dirt from one of my previous years' treasure hunts.

Counting out the eggs and neatly placing a few chocolates in each one along with a clue to the next egg, I think I had more fun planning the treasure hunts than the kids did participating in them. The very last egg held the master clue to the mother gift that was usually hidden right back in the house under their beds or in a closet.

Sense and sensibility were sometimes a big part of my downfall when it came to the planning stages of egg hiding. On an early evening before the holiday, a neatly placed egg in an open pig feeder seemed humorous and easy to find when looking over the top, but lack of judgment and hungry pigs in the morning caused the feed to disappear, along with the egg.

Our mailman loved his Easter treats the Monday after, always finding un-mapped eggs filled with chocolate treats in the mail box, and then speeding off to the next farm, thinking some idiot may have screwed up their clues also.

We had a heck of a time netting the woodpecker that was hopping around on the ground with a plastic egg stuck in his beak. Who would have thought the silly bird would try to pluck open a bright pink plastic egg in a bird feeder?

Raccoons are usually still snoozing around Easter, but one year a little bandit must have been following me while I was dispensing the treasure clues, as sometime later we found her hideout with five or six plastic eggs neatly opened and all the chocolate missing.

Pointing to the eggs and saying "no" to the dog was a silly delusion. Dog sat back and watched, behaving better than Lassie, until after dark when I was inside the house. Easter morning, dog sat outside the house wagging his tail, a heaping pile of treasured plastic eggs at the bottom of the steps. Yeah, smart dog; I suppose he read the clues inside too.

Ed didn't talk to me until the Fourth of July after the 1990 Easter egg hunt. Using real hard-boiled eggs that year, I didn't give it a thought that it might not be a good idea to hide a few of them in his pickup muffler. At least when he went to the elevator to pick up feed for the next couple of months, all the guys moved their trucks out of the way and waved him in first.

After I filled up the hay feeders in the stalls for the horses each night, each critter would eat two thirds of the way down—never more, never less. That is, until there was a chocolate-filled plastic Easter egg hidden at the very bottom, way in the back. The eleventh commandment should read, "All veterinarians shalt go to Easter sun-rise worship before attending to an ill horse and writing out the bill."

Shaped like little black birds, the realistic-looking milk-chocolate fowl with Happy Easter necklaces came ten to a package, and I had a blast placing them here and there in amongst the branches of the back trees. It took most of the day and a whole lot of energy as a ladder had to be used, as well as a lot of imagination, to make the flock seem real. I was so dang excited, it was hard to sleep as I looked forward to how the clues in the eggs for the kids the next morning would lead them to a humongous gathering of chocolate birds.

Since when did we start giving shotguns to the boys as Easter gifts, and was it really necessary for Ed to take them blackbird hunting in the back trees at dawn?...

For the Record

Right before the "I do's," it is strongly advised that all gals marrying a farmer sign an "I don't" clause that ensures any planned participation in outside activities be agreed upon in advance by both parties. It should specifically be stipulated that no harm of any kind will come to the wife or any of the wife's limbs while working with machinery or livestock. A copy of this simple little form ought to be permanently magnetized on the refrigerator door and taped to the wall behind the toilet to be reviewed daily by the farmer.

When harvest help is needed and a driver is selected to pull a 30-foot trailer loaded with a combine header down a narrow, two-lane highway, don't tell the wife she's the only one available to do the job. This places the pony-tailed partner in a predicament of either saying "no" — thus creating major hostilities between the associates — or "yes" and being splattered all over the road, enacting the Catch-22 law.

An agreed-upon arrangement of two hours helping the farmer spray a field by walking the edges as a human marker is null and void after five hours. For an analogy, consider that three extra hours of bread-rising makes for a very messy kitchen as the dough oozes through the oven door.

A strict contract must be enforced when the female of the farming partnership is asked to lend a hand around heavy machinery in the shop. Farmers should be required by law to compensate for the curiosity of the wife. For instance, a floor jack holding up the front end of an "out of order" grain truck has a hair trigger. Women adore sparkly objects, and it's in their nature to touch them "just a little bit." Poof! — a negligence complaint is filed by the farmer, and the insurance agent doesn't believe for one minute that "the dog did it."

Creative incompetence is explained at its best while driving a tractor with a digger tagging behind down a gravel road. Third-party witnesses are required to explain how the digger, by some unexplained phenomenon, was lowered onto the road for half a mile, forcing the county maintenance personnel to file a Section 8. In this instance, the shiny-button rule should seriously be acknowledged.

"I quit" is immediately overruled by "you can't" when sorting and loading pigs. Challenging any appeals, the "Sunset Provision" prevails each and every time. After so many years of working side by side, Ed and I have everything down to a tee, except irritation and aggravation. Ed hooks the trailer up while I read my e-mail. Ed is irritated I'm not out the door in time, and I am agitated that the World Wide Web and the rest of my coffee have to wait for a few hours.

Markers? Check. Rubber boots? Check. Sorting boards? Check. Patience? Not checked. My job is to run the little door that categorizes the lighter porcine from the heavier. Ed works outside marking the selected pigs, using a spray bottle filled with colored ink while shooing them towards the door. Red ink is his choice for the day, but it doesn't show up well on black pigs. It's a little dark on my side of the jobsite inside the barn, and a couple of marked porkers are mistakenly let back through the door.

"Emily, [nasty verbiage,] I'm not chasing them in just so you can chase them back out again!"

"Ed, [nasty verbiage,] if you used a lighter-colored marker, I could see which of these four-footed pork chops are supposed to stay in!"

Loud language doesn't help much around a huge group of pigs, and they all come charging towards my little swinging door. Backed up into the wall joists, I face certain death via spare ribs and ham hocks. It's not a one-time occurrence; the wall joist safety partitions are used at least twice during each loading. My part of the job is like a giant foosball game; opening and shutting the little door requires speedy reflexes and sometimes almost semi-unintelligent fun.

When the pigs are loaded and the trailer door is latched, Ed offers me coffee from his thermos and I wish him a safe trip to the stockyards (pending his execution)…

Camels Have Humps; Llamas Don't

Dad was a trader of sorts and brought home all kinds of interesting things. The day he brought home a llama really messed up my happy little animal kingdom.

Riding home on the school bus, I always looked forward to seeing my horses grazing in the front pasture as the bus pulled up. That particular day the horses were nowhere to be seen and, standing alone at the middle of the fence, was a hideous looking camel without a hump. In a tizzy as to where the horses were and what this "thing" was doing in their space, I confronted Dad. "Oh, no problem," he said, "I traded a shotgun for the llama and it kind of spooked the horses and they ran off."

Well, finding horses was first on the list, and then I moseyed out for a meet-and-greet with the new fellow to see just what was so scary about him. All the horses grouped together in the corner, watching to see if I would be eaten alive and ready to jump fence again at any moment.

As we eyed each other up, the lama didn't look too terrifying. His eyes were kind of pretty, and standing there looking like a rag-doll miniature camel, he didn't seem too threatening.

His hair was all matted and smelly, so I thought a quick brushing would make us jolly good friends in a hurry.

Oh my, was that a mistake! Llama started making a funny noise in his throat while putting his head way up and back, and then — "splewie" — I was spit on with gunk that smelled worse than rotten goose eggs.

That little kindergarten antic immediately ended our friendship, and I went crying to Dad to please remove the fake camel from my horses' pasture.

Back then, no one in the county had ever even seen a llama, much less sported one on their property, so Dad was a little miffed that he couldn't display the new creature out in the open for all the neighbors to gawk at. "Get a halter and we'll put him in the barn" was a lot easier said than done. We both found out in a real hurry why the horses took off — Llama viewed everything that walked, no matter if they had two legs or four, as a "female llama." While Dad was being "prospected and circled" by his newfound pet, he yelled at me to run and grab a long rope, but I couldn't move; it was the most hilarious thing I'd ever seen, and I was laughing so hard I was crying.

Mom came down to see what all the commotion was about, and Llama must have viewed her as a delicacy as she made a fast U-turn, running for the house with him loping close behind. Losing her apron and slippers, she made it inside the house just in time as the llama circled the front porch. Out the kitchen window came a spiel of swear words at Dad I had never heard before, and he just stood there with his mouth open — it was great!

Llama was placed in "solitary confinement" in the extra cow pasture by the river and seemed happy enough by himself. We didn't see any sign of squirrels or coon around there for a long, long time.

About a year later, the neighbor from across the river came to say a cow of his was stuck in the mud on our side of the bank. He asked Dad if it was OK to go down there to get the cow out, and with a raised eyebrow and a smirk, Dad said, "Sure, go ahead."

For as long as I can remember, this neighbor and Dad didn't care for each other too much. I think it all started when Dad was aiming at a varmint and shot the window out of the neighbor's pickup from our side of the river.

This was going to be good — better than fireworks on the Fourth of July — as Dad and I pretended to fix a fence within eyesight of the river bank and the extra cow pasture. There was only one way in and out of the pasture, so we lollygagged around by the gate, waiting as the neighbor's head disappeared over the edge of the river bank. About five minutes later, we could hear the fellow hollering, and over the bank he came a-running with his shirt half torn off and Llama close on his heels.

I've never seen anyone clear a gate like he did and keep running without missing a step! In passing, we heard him yell something to the tune of "Keep the %&*# cow! You people have a he-devil, vomiting deer in your pasture!"

Dad traded the llama off in a big hurry before the sheriff showed up. I never did find out how the deal went down, but it was awesome to see Mom's face through the kitchen window as Dad walked up with the box of tame baby skunks...

Dry Clean Only

Washing a load of clothes around here is no big deal, unless you're rinsing a load of whites and, as they're taken out of the washer, little bits and pieces of straw are stuck all over them. In the bottom of the washer lie a jack knife, a ballpoint pen, and a tape measure. "EDDDD!" I get an "Oh, sorry about that" in passing, but he's not sorry; his clothes are clean.

How can a man figure out how many ounces it takes "divided by pi" to spray an entire section of land, or be able to replace or repair every part of a pickup engine, but can't remember to clean out his pockets before washing a load of clothes?

Categorized according to dirt and smell, Ed's work clothes range from grubby to disgusting to downright un-washable. A pair of coveralls coming from the pig barn are dirty and stinky but cleansable. That same pair of coveralls coming from a newborn-calf delivery are disgusting, but the coveralls that come from the shop after rolling around in the grease and then going through the livestock barns for a week are un-washable. Negative on that load of laundry; it goes to takeout.

I deliver the un-washables to a secret Laundromat. Mr. Fischer is a very kind, retired farmer who washes by the pound. He doesn't seem to mind the grease and smell and, at the same time, doesn't seem to care that everyone who had been in his establishment before I arrived was now exiting.

Years ago, I was late for a banking appointment in town and, while leaving, decided to take a quick tour through the barn to make sure all was OK with the newborn pigs. I was used to the aroma that immediately saturates your hair and clothes and didn't think anything of it.

As I chatted with a young gal while waiting for the banker, she seemed kind of "stuck up" and moved a ways away. My turn in the banker's office was amazingly swift; papers were offered to be "sent out" to sign; I didn't get the "ho-hum" about being responsible for money spent, and was presented a free toaster while being ushered out the door. Mr. Banker had apparently suddenly come down with an allergy of some kind as he was holding a hanky under his nose and breathing kind of funny.

Back in the pickup, my hair was a muss so a quick run-through with a comb was in order. Oh my, something smelled like pigs, and there were certainly no passengers with me in the cab! Pondering the situation, I thought, "What the heck," — being it was two weeks from Christmas and the Wal-Mart checkout lines would be intolerably slow — "let's try a little fast-forward experiment!"

Walking into the store, I felt a little bit like "Pigpen" in the Charlie Brown story, eyeing up everyone that came close to see if my invisible protection would fend off the mob.

Not really needing anything, I spotted a white Christmas sweater with a little red Santa embroidered on the front; it would be perfect for the holiday festivities. I headed for the checkouts for the big test. Twenty grumpy persons were in the line I chose with the end gentleman saying to his wife that he had forgotten to buy shaving lotion and would be right back. The wife followed, rolling her eyes at me, and ignored my question of what would look better with the sweater — red or black boots?

Two young men were next in line, and as I was thinking they could both use a pair of suspenders for Christmas, they made a hurried getaway for the video department.

One by one the customers peeled away, making their excuses, until I arrived at the counter. This was the quickest way to clear out a crowd that I'd seen since Uncle Curt overindulged in hard-boiled eggs and beer at Thanksgiving! The checker didn't ask for my driver's license and the "greeter" held open the automatic doors for me on the way out.

My new sweater had to be washed as a little aroma had brushed off on it, and in my hurry, I forgot to check the machine first. Santa came out with a day's growth of yellow straw whiskers...

Concealed by Default

One of my "to me from me" Christmas presents this year was a brand-spankin'-new, double-decker, clear-glass cookie jar with a non-skid bottom and unbreakable lid. It was really hard to toss the old one, but the amount of Super Glue that was holding it together had started to stink up the goodies inside.

Oreo cookies looked beautiful in the new jar, all placed in neat little stacks or swirls, depending on the day of the week and whether I thought my kitchen should look modern or contemporary.

Oreos and I have a love-hate relationship; it's one of those snacks that reach out and grab you from inside the jar while you pass by and nag until not just one hand is full of cookies, but both, with a couple extra for the pockets.

The black-and-white beauties have a way of making one's mouth water from twenty miles away, and by the time a person is pulling into the driveway, it's a beeline straight to the jar. Not having bought replacement Oreos that day as there should have been more than enough to go around until the next shopping trip, I sank right down to the kitchen floor as the cookie jar sported just a few black crumbs. Almost to the point of having to go to counseling while imagining stack after stack of shiny Oreo packages back at the store, I high-tailed it back to town for a supply of my very own.

Oreos fit nicely in the quarter slots of the car's console. There's also a "liver" stamp in the junk drawer that, when inked on a white paper-wrapped bundle of Oreos in the freezer helps them remain Emily's very own hidden treasure, as no one in our house likes liver and would ever notice the package got a bit smaller each day. One whole package of Oreos fits perfectly in the vacuum cleaner hose and, God forbid, if someone turned it on, they would disappear unnoticed into the depths of dust.

Some items that I've hidden so well I just plain forgot about them have been happened upon and have gotten me into a big pile of do-do. I think the worst instance was when my oldest son brought home a nasty video and stashed it under his mattress, never in a million years thinking that Mom would wash his sheets each Saturday. Deciding to teach the boy a lesson, I seized the video and placed it behind some brushes in the back of a cabinet in my horse barn. I fully intended to wrap the video up as a wedding gag gift a thousand years later, but my little plan backfired when Ed found it. Now, Ed borrows my hammers, my ladder, and sometimes even a straw bale or two, but what was he thinking, going into the cabinet in my barn for a brush to beautify the dog? Oh, holy Hannah, did I ever have some explaining to do!

Saving a dollar here and a dollar there, I wasn't saving for a new pair of shoes at the end of the month; after four years, I brought home a shiny new stock trailer. After Ed came down off the ceiling — and, believe me, it took a couple of weeks — he hooked the trailer up and hauled a load of pigs in it. After the second or third load, I caught a grin and even received a little nod when I passed him on the road. Totally backfiring, my plan to haul Ol' Dobbin in a nice new, clean trailer went out the window and down the smelly trail.

Ed really jumped when I told him he had some brown stuff smeared on his face. Figuring it was just dirt, I went about my business until, a few days later, the same smudge was showing on his chin. A bit suspicious, I didn't say anything and let him fall asleep in the recliner while watching the nightly news. Sneaking over and taking a whiff of the smudge, I found it was just as I thought: chocolate!

Ed had hauled a load of livestock the week before and had made his usual stop at Fleet Farm for feed stuff, lumber, or whatever his little grocery list entailed, but chocolate not brought into the house was against our wedding vows.

Rifling through the pickup inch by inch with a flashlight at midnight, I found things I never knew existed and that Ed probably didn't either, but alas, no chocolate. Leaving the lights off in the shop, I felt like the main character in Watergate with my Mini Mag flashlight leading the way to Ed's chocolate stash. The more I searched, the more the "chocolate" spot in my brain dug in and said, "Feed me."

Just before dawn, thinking I could straighten the shop up after a nap before Ed found everything inside out and upside down, I found the mother lode under the seat of the riding lawn mower. Chocolate stars, hundreds of them! I sat atop the mower seat, enjoying every morsel star by star, and it was fully daylight by the time I waddled across the yard and into the house. Ed was sitting at the kitchen table sipping coffee and asked what I was doing outside so early. "Oh, just checking on a mare that's due to foal soon," I said, thinking, "What's he looking at?" as I headed down the hall to the bathroom with a very queasy stomach. One look in the mirror brought Lucy Ricardo to mind as I viewed chocolate-star evidence smeared all over my face...

Captain Crunch-Berries Strikes Again

In recent years, some of my most vivid memories have come about while enjoying a bowl of my favorite cold cereal.

Some crunchy recollections involved realizing my home was hopelessly overrun by Asian beetles, along with a solar eclipse and an instant igloo in the middle of the winter caused by a very, very large, misdirected tractor snow blower.

I was down to the last berry in the bowl some years ago in early April when a very bad memory started as Uncle Curt burst into the house screaming that we needed to fill our water jugs right away. Water jugs? Yep, Uncle Curt informed us that our beautiful snowfall was predicted to turn to rain, then sleet accompanied by a strong north wind that would topple the power poles in no time at all. Water jugs? Ed was already out the door when it dawned on me that, without power, the well would not function and, thus, no water would be available to wash cereal bowls. What I didn't know was that we should have filled both bathtubs, the sinks, the trunk, the extra fish tank, and anything else that would have held a drop or two.

The day before had brought above-normal temperatures with more grass showing than snow, so the spring ceremony of removing the heater from the horses' water tank and sweeping out the barn commenced. Sorrel boots were packed away and replaced by rubber ones while the purple-and-green-striped Dr. Seuss stocking hat with the orange ball on the end was switched for my favorite baseball cap.

Usually it's a loud or strange noise that wakes a person up in the middle of the night, but this time it was the silence—cold and pitch dark. Obviously, we had lost power, so I stumbled out to the front window to see who else around the county was without light. Finding the window was a surreal experience; it was pitch dark on the inside and darker than that on the outside of the house. No yard lights, no lights glowing from the nearby town, nothing. "ED!"

After a nice little "you had it last; no, you had it last" argument about where the flashlight could be found, I went back to bed, leaving Ed with a candle that would hopefully melt in his hand.

Looking out the door at daylight, I counted on one finger the power poles left standing as far as a person could see. Dang, we would never ever hear the last of Uncle Curt's "I told you so's."

As the saying goes, "When a chicken lays an egg, fry it."

Ed had dropped off a propane heater for the kitchen and then disappeared to tend to the livestock. I figured out that a thin frying pan placed on top of the heater cooked anything I wanted, even over-easy eggs.

After a few days of melted snow for washing, and cooking with my little propane life saver, the attitude in the house resembled farting in a submarine.

Wanting to tear my hair out while staring out the window for hours on end, waiting for the power truck to light up our lives, I decided it was time to break away for a day.

Didn't the shoppers at the electric-powered Wal-Mart realize I had come into the store from the depths of doom twenty miles away for a little merriment and perfume testing? Two ladies were just about pulverized by my cart as they argued over a frilly undergarment on sale while I was shopping for flashlight batteries, candles, and nonperishable foods. My find of the century was a black-and-white, teeny-tiny, battery-operated television way back in the corner thrift aisle. Awesome! — the power problem was immediately secondary as I could now lounge on the couch watching "The Young and the Restless," nibbling on my nonperishable, five-pound box of leftover Valentine chocolates!

When I treated myself to a very large takeout at McDonald's on the way out of town, the young lad behind the counter seemed a little nervous and confused by my request of a supersized number three power pole truck.

Back home, it was a little frosty in the house, but a surefire cure was a few blankets, handfuls of outdated chocolates, and a long-awaited soap opera.

There are no juicy, Emmy-award-winning soaps on the public broadcasting channel, the only station that would materialize with a little fuzz around the edges and a good shake of the tiny television. Sinking back to submarine mode, I watched a three-hour special with breaks for fundraising—a documentary on how electricity was made.

I suppose my grandchildren will wonder why the family album includes several 8–by-10 glossy photos of power trucks at the end of our driveway replacing the poles…

"You're Hired"

The two sweetest words a fifteen-year-old gal could ever hear! Cleaning stalls, grooming, and feeding horses at a local horse trainer's wouldn't be a job; it would be paradise! With a horse around every corner and maybe even a chance to ride a few that didn't dump me off every five minutes like ol' Ranger the Terrible at home, life could never, ever get any better.

When I announced to the family that I would be working after school each day, Dad had to get a little realistic and rain on my parade by asking how it was that I would be transported to and from my new place of employment.

Just a little technical difficulty I hadn't thought of; after all, what teenager thinks past their nose, much less plans a day or a week ahead?

It was recommended that "Old Blue" be my mode of transportation, and, looking back, I suppose Dad figured if I were going to wreck a vehicle, I couldn't do much more harm to the truck than my brothers had already done.

Old Blue was a -"he" — at least that's what Dad called the truck when it ran decent. "He'll take me through the swamp, or he'll pull the tractor out of the mud." Mostly held together by a roll of barbed wire and two-by-fours screwed on the sides in place of long-lost fenders, Old Blue was an embarrassment by anyone's standards, much less as a young gal's first Cadillac workmobile.

Despite the lack of paint and body parts, the apprentice position and beautiful horses on "the other side of the fence" outweighed any crude stares or smug comments that might come along. So I agreed in a flash to drive the old beast to and fro.

Not quite the get-in-and-go type, Blue's driving mechanism consisted of a clutch and a three-speed shifter on the column. There was no D for drive, or R for reverse — just a "wannabe blinker" on the right side between the steering wheel and the dash.

As I received the quick-shifting tour from Dad, he explained that first gear was "up here," second "down there," and third gear "up an' over that way." He made it clear that reverse was towards yourself and straight down, but his "Do you understand?" went in one ear and right out the other as my mind was on grooming a hunter-jumper at my new place of employment.

All shined up with jeans tucked inside my boots, I was off the school bus and in the truck lickity-split, shaking my head at actually getting paid for a job I would have done for free.

Now, where did Dad say first gear was again? If Old Blue would have had a side window, I would have banged my head against it for not listening closer to the shifting instructions, but with no one around, I was on my own.

I figured if I could just find first gear, slow going would be just fine as my new occupation was just a few miles away. Up and over? Over and down? Sliding the shifter into a gear position that seemed right, I let the clutch out as the "chug chugs" advanced Blue about ten feet. As I tried again, my head bounced from the back window to the steering wheel and back again in a pattern I will never forget since the "chug chugs" lasted a good thirty feet.

After a momentary thought of saddling up Ranger the Bronc for transportation, I figured my time was better spent finding the gears than face down in the dirt.

A mere half-hour later and suffering from a humongous headache, I was out the driveway and down the road to employment bliss.

First gear wasn't bad as the slow going allowed me to see, up close and personal, what the rear end of a skunk looked like just before the little black and white beauty sprayed Blue's tires.

Passing the swamp that Dad drove through to chase in the cows, I wondered if he'd ever seen the monster snapping turtle which kept right up with me alongside the road, threatening to chew Old Blue to pieces.

As I pulled up to cross the highway, the teenage "not thinking past the nose" theory kicked in real fast. With cars and semis passing in both directions, I was about as stuck as stuck could be, wondering how the heck I would get through the "chug chugs" to cross without being smashed to oblivion.

By this time, I couldn't care less if twenty of the state's most well-trained champion horses waited at a stable for me just a mile away. Pretending to fix my hair in the mirror, I smiled and waved to passing traffic while taking a deep breath and letting out the clutch when the coast was clear. At 20 miles per hour in reverse, Old Blue took out the railroad crossing sign, the deer crossing sign, and the "curve ahead" sign all in one gigantic "chug."

With a good fifty feet of runway now between Blue and the highway, it took every inch as we chugged along in first gear, crossing just before a semi-load of cattle whizzed by.

It took better than an hour to get turned around and back across the highway. Blue had no headlights and I had to be home by dark. Mom didn't believe I never made it to the stable and cursed my "previous employer" up one side and down the other on the phone for letting me ride a wild horse, getting nasty black and blue bruises on my forehead and huge snow cones on each side of my ponytail....

Don't Want It All

Everyone has seen the television commercial that has the jingle in the background, "I want it all, and I want it now." The wife sends her husband for a new digital TV and, on his way out the door she says, "Just don't go overboard." I thought that was the slickest deal ever and tried it on Ed, saying in passing that we needed a new lawn mower, but before I could say "Don't go overboard," he was out the door.

Mowing to me is an art. Each up-and-down row must be perfectly straight with the circles around the trees blended in neatly. A fierce fetish of mine has always been if you're not going to trim afterwards or don't have time, don't bother starting as the lawn would not be level and tidy.

I thought of counseling for my little obsession once, but nowhere in the therapy Yellow Pages is there listed a cure for "orderly lawn madness." Digging down deep, I know dang well where my little problem stems from and have never been able to talk out loud to anyone about it. It was the "three-wheeled people-eater," as we dubbed it — a lawn mower us kids used to mow the yard, the pastures, and the ditch banks.

That bugger had one handle — forward to go and back to stop. If you let go or slipped off the handlebars when running behind, it would not stop for any person, place, or thing until it ran out of gas. That's where my little "even lawn syndrome" originated as half a rosebush, half a clothesline, and half a fence just did not look very even when the "people-eater" had been set free by accident.

After fighting for the last few years, buying new blades, sharpening them to extinction, and replacing part after part for our old mower to get a half-ways even look to the yard, I finally threw my hands up and spoke those television commercial words to Ed.

Excited as all get-out to try out the new mower, I rushed through errands in town like never before to get home before dark to try out the new and improved machine. Who cared that I had come home with half a loaf of bread, half a pint of milk and a partial of the parts list? All I could think of was a beautiful, smooth, and tidy lawn that I could gaze at day after day.

As I tossed the milk in the cupboard and the parts in the fridge, there were two hours of daylight left for splendidly smooth, hassle-free mowing! Grabbing the camera to take a picture of the glorious new machine parked beside the house, I was in seventh heaven! Ignoring the note that Ed had left on the steering wheel—"See Ed before mowing"—I hopped on while marking the day and time my dreams had come true.

Headlights! Heck, I would be able to mow all night long! A big bumper around the front—OK, OK, I guess that would save some of the tree bark. A horn? OK, Ed, that can be your funny as I pressed it and fell right off the back; an air horn was a bit much! I'm not sure how many beverages one person can drink at a time, but four cup-holders was a bit eccentric. A twelve-volt plug-in—how lovely; my portable DVD player would fit very nicely propped against the dash. Cruise control? Now, Ed, you know dang well I've never been stopped for speeding in my entire life and I sure wasn't going to risk being pulled over by the lawn police.

Starting the engine, I had to wipe away tears as there was no back-fire or "clunk, clunk" noise—just a powerful, smooth-running hum. Looking around, I noticed that also missing was a "Go" lever, clutch, and blade engager. All I could find was a suspicious-looking pedal on the right that, when pressed with my foot, took the front of the mower right off the ground. ED!

The explanation from Ed was quite simple. Automatic hydrostatic, self-leveling, speed up, slow down all in one simple foot peddle. For further ease of deck leveling, the button on the right would take care of any angle desired. Diverting my attention to the lower level, Ed pointed to the hose hookup that would automatically clean the underdeck after mowing.

Now, I come from a school where there are levers to place the blade up and down. A throttle handle usually makes things go faster or slower and I'll be darned if a little button will make my mowing any easier while, for the life of me—a self-cleaning lawn mower?

I gazed at the neat and tidy electric fence surrounding the yard where the horses were eating all the medium grass off in one level while the cows followed, eliminating all the longer and dense turf. The hogs were doing a precise job of tidy trimming around the edges while the dog kept the whole works moving at a steady pace. At the same time two loads of dishes were being washed hydrostatically underneath the lawn mower while a load of jeans was waiting in the basket...

Snowed In

I have a love-hate relationship with snow. The little kid in me wants a couple feet of the beautiful fluffy playground material, but the mature adult side of me says, "Snow stinks!"

Waking up to ten new inches of the crystallized H2O puts one in such a joyful mood. Shoveling used to be an aerobic exercise, and if one was creative enough, initials and secret messages could be carved all over the sidewalk and entire farm. This year, I would first test myself on remembering where the shovel was, and if found, would break the handle off and shrug my shoulders while pointing to the dog.

I stuffed myself into my insulated coveralls, but the dang things wouldn't zip up again. Last spring I promised myself they would close with room to spare by this snow season; maybe next year.

The house cat did his little Garfield dance, followed by two short meows that meant he wanted outside. I told him the snow was deep and he was a foolish feline to attempt it, but out the door he dashed, totally disappearing under the snow except for his tail. The tail did a huge loop around the front yard, sticking out of the snow, and back through the front door in a matter of seconds. Shame on me, but I had to laugh, and it was a good snow moment.

These leg muscles that we must use to trudge through the fine ice crystals should be warned in advance. By the time I got to the barn to let the horses out, I was walking like Old Saint Nick himself, with no bend-ability left.

After the first heavy snowfall, I'm pretty good to remember to not kick the bottom of the barn door when opening it. Yep, down it came off the roof right on top of my head and onto the back of my neck to make a very bad and foul-languaged snow moment.

Anxious to see the weanling colt's first snow steps, I found it a fine, fine moment watching him hit the powder and do the hot-potato hop as he was eaten alive by ten inches of white wolf.

Watching the warnings and closings scroll across the bottom of the television screen, I could swear I saw that in between Eagan and Enderlin it scrolled that "Emily" was closed for the day. So be it; as I was stranded in the house, I would get out my long-lost list of "to dos" and accomplish great things.

I will never list patching jeans as number one on my resume. After breaking the third needle and sewing the legs together, it was time for a snack. All I could think of was cherry cheesecake, and according to the date on the Philadelphia package, we wouldn't be baking a pan of that today. Improvising, I crushed up graham crackers and sprinkled them on top of an open can of cherries.

Settling on the couch with my very own personal cherry-tart concoction, I tuned in to a soap opera I hadn't seen for a year. Some of the main actors were the same but married to different people. One gal was having a baby — the same lady that, a year ago, had introduced her granddaughter on the show. Bridget was baking cookies while concealing the identity of her child's father to her cousin's maid who used to be the main character on a different channel.

Those cookies looked a lot better than my cherry-tart mixture so, during the fifteen-minute commercial, I put the Kitchen-Aid mixer to work on some chocolate-chip delights. Finding no chips in the pantry, I sat down with the mixing bowl and ate most of the dough. "Let it snow, let it snow, let it snow!"

After a breather, the next item on the list read "clean closet." Mad at myself for actually buying the containers to organize the closet items a very long time ago, I dug in. After making a big pile of "no fit" clothes, then putting them in a "maybe next year" tote, the next item I pulled out to save or toss was an electric ice cream maker Ed and I had received as a wedding gift. Blowing the dust off, I thought, "What the heck," and hauled it off to the kitchen.

Some of the directions were missing, but a stubborn, housebound woman wouldn't let a little thing like that tarnish a good bowl of ice cream!

The Abominable Snowman himself couldn't have made a bigger mess than that ice cream maker did to my kitchen. Finding out way too late that the missing directions were taped to the lid, I penciled in "wash kitchen ceiling" on the "to do" list after I finished eating what was left in the bottom of the container.

Digging in the cupboard for some rags, I discovered, there, on the very back shelf, an entire box of Little Debbie's fudge brownies. "Who can eat just one?" I thought as I sat down, immensely enjoying my little snow party moment.

Ed came in that evening and asked what was for supper. Well, dear, we're out of everything and I couldn't make it to town for groceries because of the snow; besides that, we should try to cut back…

Barn in a Bag

A friend of mine is in the planning stages of building a new horse barn. After several "can't you see it?'s" of the different layouts, my friend has taken her plans, along with my suggested changes, and run. So, when her barn is unorganized and only fits five of her six horses comfortably, I will not be offering an extra stall in my neat and tidy barn, no sir!

Dreaming of building the "perfect horse barn" my entire life, I started with tinker toys, gradually tapered into an erector set, and in the sixth grade received the blue ribbon in art class, not for etched flowers, but for an impressive drawing of a red barn with a three-rail white fence as far as the eye could see (or to the edge of the paper).

When it looked like my dream would finally materialize, I purchased a thick drafting tablet and no one in the house ate or had clean clothes for a month until the perfect horse barn plan was completed.

Using about five cans of white spray paint on the grass, I sprayed out the actual size of the barn foot by foot, complete with doors and hay storage areas. I didn't realize the particular brand of paint I was using was water-proof and soil proof, so, to this day, there's a big square of un-built barn in faded white on the north edge of our property.

Bringing my budget and plans to the builder, I soon sank very low in the chair. The automatic water spigots would have to be erased, along with each horse's personal turnout area. The builder shredded my page of connecting hay storage and penciled over the private skylights above each stall. Asking the fellow if flowers planted in front of the barn were allowed in my budget, I sarcastically drew a square box on the back of the tablet and handed over my check.

With just a few days to go until the engineers arrived to erect the world's most perfect horse barn, the site had to be cleared and leveled. As a "non-horse person," Ed argued with me long into the night about taking out an oak tree that I was sure could stay and he was sure had to be chopped down as it would interfere with the front sliding door. Saying goodbye to the image of brushing my horse in the shade, I saw that all that was left of the tree the next morning was a three-inch stump. Now, if the tree would interfere with the sliding door, wouldn't a big fat stump be just a tish problematic as well?

Seeing the huge truck coming down the road loaded with barn materials, I grabbed the camera to record in history forever and ever Emily's barn-raising.

When the workers introduced themselves as Tom and Joe while asking where to place the building, I asked right back where the heck the rest of my barn was! On a flatbed truck totaling a foot high was the entire barn package, resembling a bed-in-a-bag from Target. Producing the receipt, I showed Boss Tom the total on the bottom while pointing to the total load on the truck and asked him if he could add. The stare-down that followed was a little uncomfortable, but both fellows backed down to take a little break, sitting on what was left of my oak tree.

Assured by the builder on the phone that all paid-for materials had been delivered and my barn would soon be raised, I hesitantly gave Boss Tom the go-ahead to start.

Watching from the back window of the house, I could see right away that worker Joe was not in his element as the first post sagged to the right and then toppled over onto the oak stump that should have been a tree. Looking for Tom to crack him one, I sprained my neck, ducking as Tom walked right by outside my secret viewing window and tinkled! How dare he!

The barn was taking shape by the next afternoon. The posts were in and, from what I could measure with the level at midnight, they were straight. Using binoculars the next morning, I counted the times Joe missed a nail, denting the roof, which raised my blood pressure to new heights. When Ed suddenly asked from the doorway behind me what I was doing, I jumped and cracked my look-out window with the spy glasses, which, in turn, about put me in the emergency room with a heart attack.

Four days later, Tom tapped on the glass of my peeping window and asked for a final inspection before they left. Crawling on my hands and knees to the front door, I sheepishly looked out while pretending to dry my hands with a dish towel.

As I viewed the barn up close in the daylight, Joe shook his head and kicked the stump that should have been a tree as I hugged the closest corner.

With the delightful engineers finally out of the way, it was time to open and close the front door to show Ed how wrong he was to chop down the mighty oak. Catching the stump corner by just a tenth of an inch, the door worked fine as far as I was concerned, and we argued until the cows came home over the tree removal.

I went out at midnight with a flashlight and an ax so Ed would see the next morning that removing a tree against Emily's wishes required removing the stump as well.

It was a really, really tough phone call the next morning asking Tom to please come and repair my damage to the front barn door...

Lifeguard on Duty

New boots are a real pain (literally). By the time they're broken in, it seems they're worn out. In my case, it's always been the inside seam between the sole and the boot itself that gives way first. The first fix is electrical tape, usually lasting a month or so before the seam rips further and the Big Guns are brought in—duct tape. I'm thinking the inventor of duct tape wore a lot of boots. A good roll of tape can make a ripped pair of boots last four or five months longer if it's re-applied every other week or so.

When the style changed from a heel boot to ropers, I scoffed at the gals wearing them. What was the boot company thinking, slicing half the heel off and making a fine pair of boots so low and ugly? I bet it took me five years before I finally got up the nerve to try a pair on, but then there was NO looking back—I was hooked! Brown was definitely not the color if you wanted to wear the new "cool"-style ropers; instead they were red, black, and, yes, I even had a pair of fancy pink roper boots to match my Sunday go-to-meetin' pink-striped shirt.

When they started changing the style of my pull-on ropers to lace-ups, it took another few years before I would give in and try on a pair of those fancy dancers. They were OK, I guess, but if you were in a hurry to get out the door, it was a pain in the rump to gather up all the laces and get them tied. Cows pushing through a gate do not stop and wait for you to lace up your boots to hurry out of the house and chase them back in!

The newest style of big fat boots called Fat Baby has me completely bewildered, and now they're making cousins to the Fats called Pro Baby and Doll Baby. Is there a problem with the good old roper boots? Maybe it's like the jeans nowadays; the bottoms just keep getting bigger and bigger. I bought a new pair of my slim-and-trim-style ropers a while ago and they branded them as "Heritage" or "Vintage." Dang, am I getting that old?

Call me silly, but I've learned a quick, foolproof way to break in new boots. When I know I'll be outside all day, I toss them into the water tank for about an hour, pour the water out, and then pull them on while they're soaking wet. The boots mold right to my foot as they dry for a perfect cozy fit by the end of the day every time. This last new pair was a tish stiffer than usual (it must have been a bad cow year), so I left them in the tank to soak overnight.

After Ed started talking to me again about three days later, I learned what had happened and why I was getting the cold shoulder. He had walked out to check on critters the next morning when I was gone and noticed my sweatshirt (that I had forgotten and left on the side of the tank) floating in the middle of the water and my boots bobbing next to it, heels up. Looking back, I guess the picture surely would have resembled a drowned Emily!

This particular stock tank is three feet deep by 10 feet across, and the bottom is dark from decades of use. Ed reached in to "save" me, and his belt buckle got tangled up on the edge, leaving him dangling like a teeter-totter. Down he went head first into the water and couldn't get all the way in or back out. There he was for a very long time doing the "dog paddle," trying to keep his upper half afloat while his lower half, outside the tank, was being "closely inspected" by a bull.

Ed finally got himself turned sideways enough to get unhooked and slid head first all the way into the tank. I guess when he finally reached the floating sweatshirt and bobbing boots in the ice-cold water, he was furious after all his trouble to find out I wasn't "drowned" after all.

After I managed to quit laughing, I did thank Ed for trying to save my life. But my patent for breaking in new boots has been placed on indefinite hold...

Drivability

OK, OK, I admit that I'm a wuss when it comes to driving, especially in the winter. What's the big deal when there's glare ice and passersby have to go around my parked car on the edge of the highway, sneering at me as I wait for the sanding truck with a package of Oreos and a half-gallon of milk? That's the one time everyone is allowed to drink straight from the carton—before the milk freezes anyways.

I really like to keep the car pointed forward and all four wheels on the pavement. The drivers behind me get a little ticked off and annoyed at my slow going on ice, but I do pull off every two or three miles to let them by so they can run into the ditch ahead of me. A little slip-sliding and Emily goes right off the deep end of panic and terror.

If I had a little chat with a counselor, I think my caution problem would go all the way back to when I was ten and my sister and I braved the Bullet ride at the fair. The operator went off on a break and forgot we were on the ride, and for a good fifteen minutes we were banged around inside out and upside down in the capsule.

A few weeks ago, after our first heavy snow, the county plow was kind enough to clear our road and take out the mailbox at the same time. That part-time fellow should have gotten a speeding ticket as, in his rush to get me out of Dodge, he left our road looking and feeling like a roller coaster. There was no way I could hold even a half cup of coffee without spilling it while driving over two miles of speed bumps! The local operator did fix our nice little trail with the blade, but I think his cousin, who also uses our road, had something to do with it.

"No Winter Maintenance" is a sign that I will always obey after my one and only time of breaking the law and driving around such a sign. Ed was not a happy camper when he first buried the pickup and then a tractor, trying to pull me out.

I get a big charge out of the town drivers who zip up behind me and then race around the first chance they get, only to be stopped beside me at the next red light. Some of the drivers get really ticked off when I stretch and yawn as I wait for it to turn green.

An unbelievable road-rage incident happened to me a few years ago after I found the grand prize at the sporting goods store. It was when the Chinese first started manufacturing authentic Missouri Valley coonskin hats out of polyester.

Buying one each for my family and friends, I couldn't wait to get home to surprise everyone with my great discovery. A lady behind me started honking and flashing her lights while still in town, and by George, if she didn't follow me right down the highway, still honking and flailing her arms. Thinking the gal must have had me confused with someone who had murdered her husband, I didn't dare slow down or stop. Thankful for the oncoming traffic so she couldn't pull up beside and take me out, I ditched her on the first field road I could find, feeling bad for running over the farmer's corn.

Too overwrought to carry in my shopping bags, I just sat at the kitchen table wondering if the lady had taken my license plate number and was at the police station drawing a mug shot of me for some crime I didn't remember committing. Turning on the radio, I heard the local talk show host taking calls when a screeching PETA voice came on describing my car to a tee, saying I was transporting cats in my trunk and had smashed two of their tails while in a hurried getaway.

Huh? This was just all too unbelievable as I counted one, two housecats alive and well at my feet, knowing I would have been ripped to smithereens if I had tried to place one of the barn cats anywhere near my car!

The light bulb came on, and when I moseyed outside, it was just as I thought: two polyester coonskin tails had escaped from their shopping bag and the locked trunk and were waving for help…

General Hospital

Having the occasion to accompany a friend to an Immediate Care Clinic, I did the usual things in the waiting room: count the squares on the ceiling, scrutinize the wannabe paintings on the wall, and people watch.

Studying a pod of unruly children, it was all I could do to not reach over and dunk each one in the fish tank. Curiosity got the best of me as I observed a toddler trying to stuff a Lego into what looked like a pop machine. Looking closer, I saw no Pepsi or Diet Coke listed—just a sign that read "Insta-Med." That's all that was on the outside, except for a couple of small slot-machine-type openings on the bottom and what looked like some security code buttons. Not wanting to admit idiocy or sound too much like a country bumpkin, I asked the receptionist if the child would put the machine out of order if the Lego were to get jammed in the slot.

"Oh, no, ma'am, the Insta-Med machine is very durable and only accepts prescription slips and credit cards." Huh? A machine that dispenses medications? Totally mind-blown and thinking Marcus Welby, M.D., would turn over in his grave if he saw this contraption, I had to sit down and ponder a bit how things have changed.

I remembered a trip to the clinic many, many years ago for our grade-school checkups; we were each required to bring a sample of personal liquid and my youngest brother dropped and broke his bottle of pee in a million messy pieces all over the waiting room floor. The prescription and medication from Mom for his temper tantrum that followed was a swift wallop to his rump.

Prescribed by Dad for headaches and ailments was crushed-up aspirin with a little sugar mixed in. Talk about a gag reflex overpowering any ailment we might have had! No Power Ranger orange-flavored medicine in sippy-cups; us kids choked down the raw deal out of a tablespoon.

Medications came straight from the cow in the barn for any type of burn; butter was ol' Bess's number-one prescription.

Oatmeal mixed with water and smeared over chicken pox eased the itch and redness considerably. And to think that nowadays kids don't have to worry about that once-in-a-lifetime Oprah Winfrey facial.

Cornstarch was originally invented for diaper rash. Have a thought or two about that when eating your next double-layered, chocolate, whipped-cream-topped, frozen Dairy Queen cake.

Speaking of diapers, cornstarch also cleaned the toilet bowl after washing the cloth, not-so-disposable diapers and hanging them out to dry.

I bet the Insta-Med machine dispenses OraJel teething pain reliever for a mere ten bucks. Mom's prescription for teething was her little finger dipped in the whisky bottle and rubbed on the gums. Dad must have had a lot of toothaches.

For the sprained and sometimes broken fingers, having been sucked up into the wringer washing machine, no trip to the doctor was necessary for a cast; popsicle sticks and duct tape did the job just fine.

Cuts and scrapes did not require a trip to the emergency room for medication, nor a side trip to the toy store afterwards. One-hundred-proof iodine was poured over the "owie" if by chance your mother could outrun and catch you.

Cold and flu season did not require a trip to the general practitioner for a shot. Warm blackberry brandy mixed with a little honey was the recommendation for the house and prescribed for all ages if the bug hit. Dad must have gotten a lot of colds, too.

On the wall of the clinic there was a sign-up sheet posted for sports-physical checkups, and I never have figured that one out. Why does a kid have to have a physical to get in shape to play a game? Isn't the exercise of playing the game supposed to take care of that?

On the way home from the Immediate Care Clinic, my friend and I stopped at a grocery store, and beside the checkout was another strange-looking Mountain Dew-throwback machine I'd never seen before.

Mesmerized by two teens tapping on the screen, I watched as they viewed a selection of movies, slid in a card and out popped a DVD! Shaking my head and longing for a penny-candy aisle, I had to peek over the teens' shoulders to see if "Little House on the Prairie" was listed...

Written in Stone

The calendar says it's spring and time to tidy up the horse barn. All the various (forgotten to take in the house last fall) bottles labeled "Do Not Freeze" are sniffed and squirted to see how they fared over the winter. Chemicals and veterinary supplies are placed in groups: (1) toss because the sides have burst; (2) see how it works when needed; and (3) what the heck is this for and why did I buy it?

Cobwebs are removed with the shop vac and the refrigerator is wiped out, plugged in, and re-stocked. Yes, I have a fridge in the barn; I get more company there than in the house. The color television with VCR is dusted off and re-programmed. Yes, there's a TV in the barn and the critters and I enjoy it immensely. When I move in a 52-inch flat-screen with DVD and matching popcorn machine, my head may then be examined.

Hay bales are set in a perfect square nursery with corner nests for the arrival of new kittens. The rugs by the walk-in door are washed, along with saddle blankets and water buckets. One of these days I'll teach the horses to wipe their feet before entering the barn.

A mighty big, round, super-duper barn fan was purchased last fall on sale, and I was itching to try it out. "Not recommended for use in small barns" was on the label, but what did the manufacturer know that I didn't? Well, I found out real quick that cats can be picked up and flown around in circles while horses don't care too much for helicopters inside the barn, so the good old square-boxed models replaced the mighty fan, and Ed received an early birthday present. The pigs loved it but looked kind of funny with their ears plastered straight up and back.(Anyone remember the flying nun?)

One last project was a big crack in the cement outside the barn door. Knowing Ed had a stash of quick-set cement, I thought, "What the heck, it couldn't be any harder to mix up than a batch of cookies." The directions said to mix with part water and stir—simple enough. As much as I hated to use my freshly washed wheelbarrow, it was the only thing big enough I could find, and I figured, since the cement mixed with water, it should easily rinse out sparkling clean before drying too hard.

Pouring in the proper amount of mix to water and, at the same time, stirring the goop with a riding crop, I was soon ready to patch up the hole. Using a feed scoop to pour the cement into the crack, I mentally added "masonry executive" to my resume. Of course, the horses' names had to be neatly inscribed along the edge and the dog had to have his paw print in the corner, so the job took a tish longer than expected. My riding crop was now a solid fixture sticking straight up out of the wheelbarrow, and the tire was a part of the patch job as I had parked the makeshift cement mixer too close to the jobsite. Betty Crocker would never allow this much of a screw-up, and neither would I.

Carefully chipping away the cement around the tire with a hammer and screwdriver while mentally adding "sculpture carving" to my cover letter, I was just a little ahead of myself before it exploded.

Standing back to survey the damage, I found that sometimes cement doesn't dry quite evenly. My boots were now a permanent part of the patch job, and slipping out of them was a heck of a lot easier than trying to walk with cement slippers. Unbalanced, I grabbed the side of the wheelbarrow, tipping what hadn't dried yet all over my stocking feet. Hanging the socks over the water hydrant handle wasn't such a good idea but, on the other hand, added some nice permanent length and leverage.

As I was leaving for town, Ed was pulling in and asked where I was headed. "Oh, I was just doing a little landscaping and thought I'd pick up some flowers to place in the nifty new boot planters in front of the horse barn."

Driving off, I was also desperately hoping to find the same exact make and model of wheelbarrow to replace the one now buried way out back in the trees...

"Dear Dad..."

If you're reading this, it means I'm still in one piece and the wheat combining is finished for the year.

That first morning, Ed and the other guys said the harvest moon would be showing up any night, and they were right. What they didn't deliberate on was that it would turn them into a bunch of wild-eyed metal junkies at the first sight of a combine.

We were off to a great start for our very first harvest together until Ed's water jug sprang a leak as he went out the door. The little trail of water went all the way out the driveway with him as it leaked through the hole in the floorboards of the truck. Someday, maybe he'll buy himself a Stanley thermos.

When I brought lunch out to the field, I had filled up a couple of empty milk cartons with water as I knew he would be pretty dry by then, but I guess in my hurry they didn't get rinsed out very well. Ed's color was back to normal by the time he came home that night.

Dad, did you ever drive a combine in your sleep? I'm pretty sure that's what Ed was doing—at least, I hope so. If the clutch was on the far left, he was having a heck of a time with that, and I'm pretty sure his right foot was holding the gas steady, but when he braked, he mumbled some awful things about a timing chain while jumping up and chasing some poor fellow named "Part" right down the hallway.

Please don't tell Mom that I'm cheating on hot lunches for the field. I know she always brought you and the rest of the crew fresh casseroles with homemade bread, but, honestly, I don't know where she found the time to do it all. A real nice fellow named Brad came along a couple weeks ago selling used books from farm to farm, and after hearing my story of time shortage and cooking, he produced a recipe paperback titled "Field Lunches on the Go." Holy cow, what a time-saver! My favorite chapter is on canning anything in the cupboard, with leftovers to boot. I did get a comment from Ed that yesterday's hot beef sandwiches tasted a little leathery, but he and the other guys were happy as all get-out when I produced a pan of five-minute short-stacked rum cake. The combines were driving a little crooked for a few rounds, but the men all had smiles on their faces.

Helping with the livestock chores during harvest was a little tough. We have a mean old bull in the north pasture, and when I went out with the corn trailer to dump a few buckets each day as Ed had instructed, the bull wouldn't let me out of the pickup. It was pretty easy to climb out the window and over the cab to toss the grain out, but one time the bull got a bit too close to the pail and ended up catching the handle on his horn. I wasn't going to argue with him—he could keep every pail on the whole dang farm if he wished, as long as it was ten feet away from me—but that mean old bugger got me in huge trouble by taking the pail and the whole herd through the fence and straight out to where Ed was combining. When you and Mom visit for Christmas and Ed takes you out to see his combine, please don't say anything about all the scratches and missing paint.

I know this letter is getting a little long and you are busy, but I have to tell you about the little incident with the neighbors' combines.

Ed and Uncle Curt call them the "fancy pants guys," as they must always have the newest and greatest line of machinery. When we were finishing up lunch one day and taking a rest in the shade of the tires, the neighbors were in the very next field and, I swear, they skipped ten rows just so they could come by us with their magnificent, sparkling equipment covering us with dust. As we scrambled to take cover from the chaff of their super-steeds, Uncle Curt reached for the shotgun behind the seat of the pickup but ended up not needing it. The harvest moon must have affected the neighbors' brains along with their arrogance as, when Fancy Pants #1 turned his combine to the left, his show-off partner made a quick turn to the right. Both Ed and Uncle Curt could barely climb into their combines as they were laughing so hard at the two show-offs' steel headers gobbling each other right up! I wished I had an instant camera in my pocket! When we visit at Christmas, I'm sure Ed will tell you the entire comical story, more than once.

Say hi to Mom…

Love, Emily

About the Author

Tammy Finney grew up on a farm with five brothers and sisters. "Our playground," she states, "was anywhere our imaginations took us, including rooftops, rivers, and haystacks."

She now lives with her husband Wayne on a working grain and livestock farm in west-central Minnesota. They have two sons, Tyler and Dustin.

Tammy is a regional sales manager and assistant managing editor for The FM Extra newspaper. Her weekly column, "The Outhouse," came about almost by accident in 2005 and has gained a devoted following.

In addition to writing, Tammy enjoys drawing, oil painting, and caring for the collection of various animals in her barn, which is never empty.